Cricket and All That

'There is no talk, none so witty and brilliant, that is as good as cricket-talk.'

Andrew Lang

Cricket and All That

*Denis Compton and
Bill Edrich*

Pelham Books
London

*The authors would like to express
their thanks to Hayters for their
help with this book.*

First published in Great Britain by
PELHAM BOOKS LTD
52 Bedford Square
London WC1B 3EF
1978

ISBN 0 7207 1101 0

Printed in Great Britain by
Billing & Sons Ltd.,
Guildford, London & Worcester

Contents

Illustrations

*The authors and publisher are grateful to the
Press Association Ltd for permission to
reproduce the photographs*

Preface

Compton and Edrich...these names in unison still excite those who remember their batting deeds, especially in that glorious summer of 1947. Rarely in the long, eventful story of the game have two players so dominated one season. In cold statistics Denis Compton scored 3,816 runs and 18 centuries; Bill Edrich 3,539 runs and 12 hundreds.

Physically and in technique at the crease they provided sharp contrasts. Compton seemed always a boyish figure in his approach to batting. The orthodox and the impudent stroke came all alike to him. Edrich lacked his partner's spontaneity, even his charisma, but no one would question his vibrancy at the wicket. Though short in stature, he yielded not an inch to the great fast bowlers of his time. Few, indeed, drove them with such belligerence.

Compton and Edrich arrived at Lord's as groundstaff boys in the thirties and each remained in the first-class game until the late 1950s. Between them they took part in a hundred and seventeen Test matches and scored a total of more than 75,000 runs.

But such memorabilia never appealed to them. They saw themselves as entertainers in a sport meant to be enjoyed by participants and public alike. Since their retirement 'the Middlesex twins', as they were affectionately dubbed, have remained close and faithful observers of cricket's changing scene. Now they have renewed their partnership and the fun they found in the game runs through this partly nostalgic yet wholly perceptive look at more than forty years among its principal personalities.

1

When we were young

I Denis Compton

Cricket is infinitely more sophisticated today than when I came into the first-class game in 1936. The development of jet travel has shrunk space to such an extent that touring sides leaving England can touch down in the Caribbean in about the same time as it once took me to travel from Lord's to Sheffield for a match against Yorkshire.

The organisation of the game has also advanced dramatically. Sponsorship has created a new source of capital and with it has come a series of exciting new competitions to encourage enormous spectator appeal. The game at Test and county level has become increasingly more lucrative and, if 'player-power' has threatened the fabric of cricket, the revolution has also served to strengthen the hand of the cricket authorities across the world.

Coaches of the calibre of Keith Andrew and Les Lenham, appointed by the National Cricket Association to comb the country for talent, are already discovering fine prospects, and television, radio and newspapers continue to play a major part in enhancing the game's popularity. The future has rarely seemed so bright.

I am often asked whether I would prefer to have played cricket in modern times. The answer is yes, because of the greater opportunities available to young players today. Of course I wonder how many times world-class fielders like Graham Barlow and Alan Ealham would run me out in the course of a season of Gillette, Benson and Hedges and John Player one-day matches. Yet, paradoxically, I have one major reservation about cricket today compared with that of yesteryear. I am not sure whether I would have gained so much pleasure from the game as I did in my career between 1936 and 1957. So in reflecting on my early life in cricket I want to stress the importance we placed on one commodity that is largely missing from the game today - the *fun*. If nothing else, I want to encourage players to enjoy themselves and restore humour and laughter to a game that has become forbiddingly serious. I attended a dinner recently at which a county captain addressed the room as if he were making a grave ministerial announcement about world famine. You would never have believed that his side had just won a major competition.

Professional cricket between the two world wars and in the immediate post-war era was a haven for colourful characters who seemed to enrich the game either with their humour or their eccentricities. I am not saying they were better men than today's generation but many were larger than life, perhaps remembered more for a funny remark at Old Trafford or an antic at Taunton than for a marvellous innings. Some were lovable, others could be unbearable, but none could be ignored. This was reflected in the way they played the game. There were bigger hitters, more fluent strokemakers and a wider variety of bowlers, and sixes seemed to sail out of grounds more often than today. There were men of extremes, some extravagant in praise and kindness, others austere, intimidating and utterly scathing if crossed. But somehow they all seemed to blend into a unit when they took the field. The prime objective then was to entertain and enjoy the game. My concern today is that the welfare state and the general levelling out has encouraged a standardisation of technique and attitude detrimental to first-class cricket. In short, some of the old spirit is missing.

My entire career seemed to be influenced by remarkable men from the moment I joined the groundstaff at Middlesex in 1932. My cricket life was made possible by two giants of sport – Sir Pelham Warner, the former

England and Middlesex captain, Test selector, tour manager and president of MCC who lived to the age of ninety, and Herbert Chapman, who made Arsenal the best football club in the world in the 1930s.

Dad was delighted when the then Mr Warner invited me to join the staff at Lord's after I had scored 112 for the London Elementary Schools against C.F. Tufnell's XI at Lord's. My mother thought otherwise. 'It's all right for four months but what's he going to do for the other eight?', queried mother, who wanted me to be a clerk at Hendon Town Hall. 'More security, better prospects', she argued. She appeared to have won the day until Herbert Chapman said he would also take me on the groundstaff at Highbury. So I joined two of the greatest sports establishments in the country at the lowest possible level. At Lord's I was the most junior member of the groundstaff. At Highbury, just as lowly. My heart would sink on Mondays as I stepped off the workmen's underground tube from Hendon to survey the scene at Arsenal. Newspapers, cigarette packets, paper bags, orange peel, comics . . . . You name it, it would be there to be picked up from the terraces.

Lord's was a little more civilised. Spectators seemed to carry most of their rubbish home, and there top priority was given to work on the pitch. If there is a finer exponent of the sweep with a besom than me, let him stand up and be seen. Manual work took precedence over cricket. Yet we received more than an hour's cricket instruction each day from the Lord's coaches George Fenner and, subsequently, Archie Fowler. To their credit and my relief they never tried to change my style. We were taught the basic principles of batting but my somewhat unorthodox approach, developed in street cricket outside our house in Alexandra Road, Hendon, was never altered. The two coaches considered that I had the basic principles, even though my front foot rarely advanced to the pitch of the ball for a shot through the covers.

I was not even encouraged to read coaching manuals.

But I loved cricket books written by Jack Hobbs, my idol, and 'Patsy' Hendren, with whom I was to play for two seasons. I did not always understand Neville Cardus's flowery words but they remained magnificent, whatever they meant. 'He kindled ravaging fires of batsmanship, but scarcely ever burned his own fingers lighting them', was how he described Bradman.

George Fenner liked my leg sweep, a shot I was conscious of playing when in short trousers outside our front door at home. The stroke was ideal for punishing anything loose from the other lads who perfected the art of street cricket. Right to the end of my career, spectators believed it was a risky shot. But if that was a misconception, so too was the belief that it brought me most of my runs. I scored more runs on the off side than ever I did with the sweep shot. 'Isn't it dangerous hitting across the line, relying on quickness of eye for survival?', they would ask in my first season. Twenty-one years later I was still explaining that the ball was coaxed away from the wicket, not struck blindly with little regard for safety. My bat would rise towards mid-off before it dropped to squirt the ball away as if I were squashing a fly against the pitch. It cost me my wicket no more than half a dozen times, one of those dismissals occurring in my second Test, at Lord's in 1938 when Bill O'Reilly deceived me with a topspinner.

My big chance came at the age of fifteen when I played for MCC against Suffolk at Felixstowe. I scored nought in the first innings, going to the wicket in boots belonging to George Brown, the former Hampshire wicketkeeper, who was playing for us in that match. My footwork was leaden, which is not surprising when you consider I was wearing 11½ boots, three sizes too large. Mine arrived overnight – I had forgotten them in my haste to get to the match – and I scored a century in the second innings. That episode should have served as a warning, because I gained a reputation over the years for forgetfulness. Some people have bad tempers. Others are lazy. My problem has been a short memory. It nearly cost me a flight to Australia in 1977 for the Centenary

London's Heathrow Airport was already swinging when I
remembered I had left my passport in the Angel Hotel at
Cardiff. Only a mercy mission up the M4, organised by the
hotel manager, saved the day.

In my formative years at Lord's there was a feeling of
immense pride and joy at being a member of the
Middlesex staff, irrespective of whether one played for the
first team or the Club and Ground. We even cherished the
opportunity to pull a huge roller across the sacred turf.
Twelve fourteen-year-olds would hump the mighty object
over the square as if in a scene from one of those films of
Roman times. I can remember the honour of receiving a
second XI cap and sweater, an emotion probably felt by
young players today but which sometimes seems clouded
by financial considerations. Cricketers must master their
craft before they have the right to consider rewards. If
they start to play the game properly the rewards will
follow. But cricket, not money, must motivate them. An
outstanding illustration of my point is shown in the way
Clive Radley plays cricket for Middlesex. He would play
on a broken ankle if necessary to further the cause of the
county. He simply loves to play the game and this is
reflected in his cricket.

One of my first joys was to bowl to MCC members in the
nets when they came to Lord's in the evenings from their
offices. We would queue on the Mound, now the site of
the Warner stand, eagerly awaiting their arrival from the
pavilion. The sessions could be quite lucrative if you
happened to be bowling to a wealthy City man. The more
experienced Middlesex professionals would normally
choose the five-bob touches, leaving the rest of us to seek
a florin if we were lucky from the more thrifty members.
The donors of the smaller awards were called 'stumers'.

Imagine my excitement when C. Aubrey Smith, once
captain of Sussex and a Hollywood filmstar, invited me to
bowl to him. My left-armers must have suited his style, for
whenever he came to Lord's he requested 'young Compton'. Some of the other pros became rather envious of

our association because not only was he a great star, often playing military roles on the big screen, but he was also a five-bob touch. We never resented bowling to these gentlemen because, apart from the rewards, they would feed us a continuous supply of stories. 'When I played against Ranji...'; 'Trumper, now there was a hitter...'; 'Larwood had nothing on Spofforth . . .'.

It surprises me that today's players spend so little time talking cricket, seeking the opinions of ex-cricketers and reading the history of the game. I would suggest that Tony Greig's knowledge of the history of cricket and the traditions of Lord's is less than any former England captain. In my day ninety-five per cent of our conversation was devoted to cricket. As a result we absorbed a lot of information, especially about batting and bowling. I have dined with Sir Donald Bradman on many occasions, not simply to eat but to listen to the man's wisdom. The conversation at table was cricket, not his own performances but his experiences of other players' contributions. He once took the time to give me a coaching session in his hotel room on the MCC tour I made to Australia in 1950-1. I averaged just over seven in Tests in that series.

Archie Fowler was the best coaching bowler I met before the war. He would bowl at me for hours, first concentrating on the leg stump, then the middle-and-leg, and so on. 'Don't listen to the coaches who want you to get your foot to the ball. Stay as you are', he would say.

I earned roughly twenty-five shillings a week when I started, a large percentage of which would be spent at the Lido cinema, Golders Green, or the Classic, Hendon. Fast-talking, straight-shooting Jimmy Cagney was an early screen hero. Humphrey Bogart was another Hollywood great I admired.

I was down on the scorecard to bat at number 10 in my first match for Middlesex at Whitsun 1936. Big Jim Smith was promoted above me in the order when the match against Sussex started, and in retrospect 'Gubby' Allen's decision was helpful. We needed 20 for a first-innings lead when I went to the wicket. By the time I was out for 14, Gubby and I had shared a last-wicket stand of 36. Gubby was furious when umpire Bill Reeves adjudged me lbw to Jim Parks. Looking the umpire straight between the eyes, he said: 'You old cheat, Bill. That boy wasn't lbw'. To his astonishment, the umpire agreed: 'Quite right, Mr Allen. That boy will be all right, but I was dying for a pee'. Bill Reeves was second only to another umpire, Alex Skelding, the former Leicestershire fast bowler, in humour. I once asked Alex how successful his benefit had been. 'Successful?', he said. 'I'll tell you. Play began before a keen wind - and that was all. Not a soul in the ground.'

I scored 1,000 runs in my first season, finishing second to Patsy in the batting averages among the regular members of the side. Despite stories to the contrary, I did not take to cricket like a duck to water. I scored only one century in the first summer - 100 not out at Northampton - and was immature in outlook and technique.

How will I ever forget the disgrace of being dismissed from the field at Lord's by the captain, Walter Robins, after dropping a catch in the deep. 'Go off the field, Compton, and get a cap', he said. 'Never appear without one on a day like this' (the sun was blazing down). I received many dressings-down from Robbie in that first season, but the confrontations were always constructive. He insisted that Middlesex players should move at the double between overs, not only to keep the game alive for spectators but to give his side more time to win a match. We rarely wasted a second. 'Come on, smarten yourselves up', he would shout. 'Compton, don't talk to spectators. Pay attention', was another favourite. He was a disciplinarian but could make you glow with pride. We once made a valiant effort to score four hundred runs for victory against Kent after the war. I scored 150 but the run chase cost us wickets and we lost the match. I was not looking forward to meeting Robbie in the pavilion.

Suddenly he strode up, shook me by the hand and said: 'A wonderful innings, Denis. Well tried, well tried'.

He loved baiting opponents. Brian Valentine and Arthur Carr, captains of Kent and Notts, disliked his arrogance. Some of the players on the county circuit called him 'Cock Robin', rather unkindly. Sometimes his teasing of opponents could pay handsome dividends. He more or less kidded Northants to defeat in my third match for Middlesex in 1936. We were worried by the fearsome pace of 'Nobby' Clark on a responsive wicket. He bowled us out for 192 in the first innings, including Compton for a duck. Robbie went to work with a special brand of propaganda when we batted a second time. 'Nobby, the way you're bowling, you'll be worn out by August', said Robins. 'Why bowl flat out all the time? Conserve some energy. A cricket career is short, especially a fast bowler's.' 'Do you think so, Mr Robins?', replied Clark, whereupon he eased up - and we won the match. Clark took my wicket for the second time but not before I had scored 87, my highest score to date.

The Middlesex staff was stacked with characters. We reckoned if ever Jim Smith remained long enough at the crease he would score the fastest century in history. The moment arrived in a match against Kent, but Big Jim had taken so many heaves without making contact that the century took well over an hour and the record eluded him.

'Patsy' Hendren had a marvellous Cockney humour. He, above anyone, taught me the importance of footwork. I would marvel at the way he danced down the wicket to Kent's 'Tich' Freeman, whose legbreaks claimed more than two hundred wickets in a number of seasons, and once more than three hundred, but rarely Patsy's. His humour was spontaneous, never contrived. In a match at the Oval, Errol Holmes of Surrey swept a ball to long leg in the direction of Joe Hulme. Unfortunately Joe 'lost' it in the backcloth of gasometers until Patsy intervened. 'There it is, Joe', he shouted. Joe reacted, flung himself across the boundary only to discover that the 'ball' was a low-flying blackbird. The ball had hit the fence some seconds before. Surrey were our opponents in another memorable match dominated by Patsy. The occasion was his final appearance in championship cricket, at Lord's in 1937. Who but Hendren could have bowed out by scoring his hundred and nineteenth hundred for Middlesex? Seventeen thousand spectators gave him rapturous applause as he walked slowly into the pavilion after scoring 103 in the first innings. By the time he joined us in the dressing room the old boy had been reduced to tears. He wrote later: 'It is a big pull leaving the stage, as they call it; leaving the people I have played with and the camaraderie of the game . . .'.

Jim Sims was another character. And like most exponents of the art of legspinning, Jim was full of theories - which he would reveal to the world through the side of his mouth. They became even more extravagant if a class batsman was facing him at the other end. Bowling to Wally Hammond at Lord's before the war, he turned to me standing at mid-off and said: 'I'll bowl him the trap ball, Denis'. 'What's that, Jim?', I asked. 'A ball just short of a length, which Wally will hit down deep square leg's throat.' Jim bowled, Hammond hooked, and the ball sailed over Alec Thompson's head at deep square leg for six. 'Where's it gone, Denis?', enquired Jim. 'Has he caught it?' 'No, it went over Alec's head, Jim', I replied. 'Over his head? It should have hit him on the bloody head'. Jim's theories did not only apply to bowling. He would trot them out freely at conferences in mid-wicket. We shared several stands, Jim always organising tactics. 'You're going well, Denis', he would say. 'Keep it up and I'll show the bowlers the bat-maker's name.'

The departure of legspinners like Sims, Doug Wright, Eric Hollies, Tich Freeman and others is one of the saddest aspects of modern cricket. If we could restore the pace of pre-war pitches to those of today, I am sure this fascinating skill could be resurrected. Few lads even bother to master the technique in schools nowadays.

Gubby Allen, who played in twenty-five Tests for England and captained the side in eleven, was another remarkable member of the Middlesex side before the war. After a season or two in his company I understood how he managed to defy Douglas Jardine's instructions to bowl 'bodyline' against Australia in 1932-3. While Bill Voce and Harold Larwood bumped the Aussies to defeat, Allen relied on his natural ability to take wickets. No other man has done more for cricket than Gubby, as player, administrator and ambassador. If ever a man deserved a knighthood for his work for a cause it is Gubby. I admit he is not everyone's cup of tea, but my only reservation is his occasional flash of stubbornness. Once he forms an opinion, he is adamant that he is right. More often than not he is, but no argument will shake him when he is occasionally a little off beam. No man had the ability to spot talent faster than Gubby. He discovered Ian Bedford, a legbreak bowler of genuine potential, who joined Middlesex just after the war and rose to captain the county before dying tragically at an early age.

I was rather frightened of Gubby when I first played. I remember his words delivered just before I faced the first ball of my career from the legendary Maurice Tate. 'A word of advice, Denis', he said. 'This man is much faster off the wicket than anything you've ever seen before. I suggest you play forward.' The first three deliveries from Tate swooped over my middle stump as I rocked on my back foot. Gubby, scratching his head, shouted from the other end: 'My boy, what did I say? Play forward to him'.

I made my Test debut against New Zealand in 1937 a little over a year after that first innings, sharing a fourth-wicket stand of 125 with Joe Hardstaff of Nottinghamshire after England had lost three wickets for 36 runs. Our partnership started in bad light and steady drizzle - a proper baptism - but the following morning it prospered on a slow wicket. My dismissal was unfortunate, run out for 65, but for once I was not to blame! Joe drove the ball straight at Vivian and the ball glanced off the bowler's hand onto the stumps with me yards up the wicket.

I had to wait until the following summer for my first hundred in Test cricket, 102 in my first appearance for England against the Australians, at Trent Bridge in 1938. I had watched Bradman from the free seats at the Nursery End after sleeping on a camp bed at the entrance to Lord's in 1930. But this was different. Here was the man himself at close quarters. His speed of foot and eye was something to behold. People called him a machine. He was, but never boring. He played all the shots, some of them incredibly unorthodox. Very seldom did Bradman lift the ball from the turf or hook in the air to fine leg in the style of Cyril Washbrook. The Don would start the stroke a split second earlier than any batsman I saw, hitting the ball wide of mid-on. His form was superb on that tour, including the Tests. First came an innings of 144 not out at Trent Bridge, then 102 not out at Lord's, followed by 103 in a hundred and sixty-five minutes on a dark day at Headingley which one newspaper called 'Leeds' unkindly light'. The Don, for all his clinical efficiency, could be a generous opponent. He gave me a marvellous accolade after I had scored 76 not out in the second innings of the drawn Test at Lord's. He shook my hand at the wicket - and later said: 'That, Denis, was one of the best innings I've seen'.

It was that Aussie tour which taught me how to read a googly in flight. 'Watch his wrist', some of the other England players would advise if I was likely to bat against Bill O'Reilly, the Australian legspin and googly bowler, or 'Chuck' Fleetwood-Smith, whose lefthand chinamen and googlies spun viciously and lifted from the pitch. After a time, I decided to watch the ball revolving in the air after it had left their hands.

We were 1 - 0 down in the series by the time the Oval Test arrived, a match more memorable for Len Hutton's world record Test score of 364 than victory for England, who shared the rubber. His performance was the greatest feat of endurance and concentration I saw in first-class cricket. O'Reilly, who bowled 85 overs in England's innings of 903-7 declared, said afterwards: 'When he was 333 not out after twelve hours and twenty-five minutes batting, I bowled two no-balls to Len. The blighter played both of them straight back down the pitch from the middle of his bat. He was grooved and not even no-balls could disturb his tremendous self-control'. The duration of that innings, just under eight hundred minutes, meant that Eddie Paynter and I sat for hours with our pads on. 'Bet you £1 we don't get 10 between us', said Paynter, a compact and mobile little lefthander who gave both Lancashire and England marvellous service. At the end of the match, which England won by an innings and more than 500 runs, I slipped Paynter a pound note. I scored one and he was out for a duck.

That match was never forgotten by at least one Australian, Mervyn Waite, a very friendly medium-paced bowler. After I pushed O'Reilly to cover for a single, Waite bowled the straightest half-volley which I somehow contrived to miss. The dismissal was irrelevant except for the fact that I became Waite's one and only victim in Test cricket. Now, whenever I go to Adelaide, Waite is the first Australian to make contact. 'Denis, Waitey here', he will announce over the telephone. 'Coming round for a drink? I owe you one. Remember, you're my one victim in Test cricket.' He was still buying me drinks at the Centenary Test in 1977.

Ben Barnett, the former Australian wicketkeeper, never forgets that Test either. He should have stumped Hutton by a mile off Fleetwood-Smith when Len had scored only 22. Hutton went down the pitch and Barnett had plenty of time to complete the stumping but fluffed the chance.

No one was happier than Barnett when Gary Sobers broke Hutton's record in scoring 365 not out against Pakistan in 1957-8. Long after the war Barnett had told me: 'I will be glad when this record is broken, Denis. The only thing people say to me is, "Do you remember when you missed Hutton?".'

My only regret in that first series against Australia was the attitude of Wally Hammond, the England captain. I was never at ease with him then, or later, when I knew him a little better. He somehow failed to communicate, rarely discussed tactics with the side, and hardly ever congratulated players on a good performance. He gave me a roasting when I returned to the pavilion after scoring a hundred on my Test debut against the Australians. My dismissal had come when I slogged the ball into deep square leg's hands. I received a wonderful reception en route to the pavilion but in the dressing room the atmosphere was icy. 'What did you want to get out for, Denis?', boomed Hammond. 'There's one thing you must learn when playing the Australians. Never give them your wicket. Don't ever do that again.' I never got to know Hammond. The professionals were seldom invited to dine with him but his magnificent batting compensated for a shortage of charm. His 240 for England in the Lord's Test of 1938 was an innings of extraordinary grace and artistry. If I had to choose a batsman from history or the present day to demonstrate the cover drive, I would hand the bat to Hammond.

Middlesex were runners-up for the title for the fourth successive time in 1939, the side led for the first time by Ian Peebles. Bill Edrich scored seven hundreds and I made six, with a total aggregate of 2,468. 'Apart from the numerical value of this performance, the manner of its achievement stamped Denis Compton as one of the world's best present-day batsmen', said Wisden. I was flattered.

I am not sure I lived up to it in facing the pace of Martindale, Hylton and Constantine, a trio of West Indian fast bowlers who troubled many an England batsman on their tour here in 1939. It was a pity Hitler spoiled the fun.

II Bill Edrich

'Go to Lord's. That's the place to be. The eyes of those

who matter will be upon you, and you'll enjoy it immensely...'. I can hear that piece of advice as if it were delivered a moment ago, for it made sense then and in retrospect was the most valuable instruction I ever received. I was a slip of sixteen when Michael Falcon, a close friend of the Edrich family and captain of Norfolk for many years, took me aside to warn me that I was about to make a grave mistake. He had come to my parents' house in Lingwood, Norfolk, on hearing that I had written to Northamptonshire requesting a trial. I had played quite well for Norfolk and as mathematics, not geography, was my strong subject, I could not see beyond the neighbouring county in considering a cricket career.

'Oh, you don't want to go there', said Falcon firmly. 'You'll enjoy it far more with Middlesex.' I never argued, for Falcon's wisdom rivalled Solomon's. My acceptance of his very word was the product of many hours of coaching. 'What field?', he would ask as I paced out my run-up in early matches for Norfolk. 'Three slips, gully, cover, forward short leg, deep fine leg...' He would halt me abruptly. 'Are you bowling on the leg stump?' 'No, off stump, sir', I would stammer. 'Then you won't be needing a deep fine leg, William', he would say kindly. I soon learned to pitch a good line.

He arranged for me to attend a trial at Lord's at about the same time that Northants replied. Their reaction was not favourable, suggesting in a very noncommittal way that they would think about my application.

My trial at Lord's in March or April 1934 was harrowing. The day before I caught a train from Norfolk to London, I split my right hand unyoking a horse on our farm. The wound was deep but protected by heavy bandage when I walked into Lord's, with my injured hand in my pocket, determined to say nothing of the accident. No sooner had I arrived than I was facing the bowling of George Fenner, the head coach, and others. Pace, swerve and spin came down but the more determined I became, the more aware I was of blood seeping freely into my glove whenever I played a shot. 'Now have a bowl, son', suggested Fenner. I removed my gloves, shielding my hand from Fenner, but he had caught sight of the gory mess. To this day I believe that my attempt to disguise the injury helped me win a place on the groundstaff.

As Denis has recalled, our role was to learn the trade of cricket between selling match cards, pulling that roller which could have flattened a motorway, clearing pigeon droppings from the seats and removing more 'bombs' if the job was not completed to satisfaction first time. My contemporaries with the paint brush, roller, mower, broom and mop included Jack Robertson, Syd Brown, Denis, Harry Sharp and Laurie Gray, all of whom became eminently better players than they were groundsmen, under the control of dear old Harry White.

We earned about £3 or £4 a week, a wage augmented by a commission for selling match cards at county games and Tests. We ran an unofficial competition to see who could sell most cards, but neither Denis nor I distinguished ourselves in that field. I would raise enough for a couple of glasses of beer before finding a quiet seat on the ground, out of sight, from which I could watch Jack Hobbs or someone else batting in the middle. There were many occasions when I would glance up between overs to catch a glimpse of a tousle-haired colleague, later to become famous for the sweep, trying to hide like some mischievous schoolboy behind the camouflage of a daily paper. Yes, D.C.S.!

Our cricket consisted mainly of matches for MCC against schools, colleges and leading clubs in the south. I believe I batted for the first time with Denis at Beaumont College. 'What do you two do?', enquired Alec Waugh, the captain of MCC and a distinguished author. 'We're bowlers', I replied. 'Right, you go 10, Compton, and you 11, Edrich', said Waugh. The MCC innings collapsed but a rather fine rearguard battle by the tailenders saw us through, much to Mr Waugh's delight.

We travelled to matches by Green Line bus, buying a

single ticket in the hope of stealing a lift back to London in an affluent teammate's Rolls-Royce or Armstrong-Siddeley. Denis had no problem begging lifts, for even then he displayed an exceptional batting technique, always going for his shots, an enchantingly natural cricketer. His strokeplay could be irresponsible at times but George Fenner worked hard to tighten his defence without once curbing the raw brilliance.

My cricket was based on the teachings of Michael Falcon and the Gospel According to Jack Nichols, a former Lancashire and Staffordshire player, who coached me at school in Norfolk. 'Down the line of the ball is the batsman's prayer', was one of his maxims. But his method of teaching the importance of keeping the head still and getting weight into a stroke was quite unorthodox. He would bang his head into my chest, knocking me off my feet. 'If you don't put your head into it like that, you're missing all that power', insisted Jack. I soon got the message.

There was an austerity about Lord's in 1934, highlighted by the great chasm in status between the amateurs and the professionals. The junior pro was recognised as the lowest of the low, almost a feudal serf, good for kicking if business was bad. It was often: 'Edrich, go there'...', 'Edrich, get changed...', 'Edrich, go home...', 'Come here, you so-and-so...'. Life could be miserable for the sensitive youngster. I felt sorry for some MCC men who were well versed in the gentle art of snobbery but short of ability with bat and ball. How I loved to whistle a bumper past the nose of the bewhiskered Lieutenant-Colonel Ethelred Dimwitty-Smythe if he requested me to bowl to him in the nets at Lord's. A moment earlier he might have been shouting at me, but a couple of short, sharp bumpers were normally sufficient to win some peace for a week or two. Unfortunately such confounded arrogance was likely to preclude you from a tip for your efforts with the ball.

I once made the mistake of bowling a bouncer to Nigel Haig, the former Middlesex captain. He had wanted a stiff net but I had misjudged the stiffness. My bowling was remarkably uncomplicated, consisting simply of a sprint run-up and a slinging action devised to propel the ball as fast and as straight as possible over twenty-two yards. When I whistled a couple of loose ones past Mr Haig's chin the great man threw down his bat and snapped: 'Edrich, I came here to practise my strokes, not for you to practise your bloody bowling. Slow down a bit'.

I stiffened with apprehension but confess that it was Hendren not Haig of whom I took most notice. I would read Patsy Hendren's career figures in Wisden as other lads of my age consumed *Captain Marvel*. His tales of adventure overseas thrilled me, especially those of the 1929 and 1934 tours to the West Indies. 'Now we've got a moment, Bill, let me tell you the tale of Joe Small', he would say, motioning me to sit next to him. Hendren had reached 96 on the 1929 tour when Small, a West Indian bowler, sidled up to him and said: 'Musser Hendren, if I get on to bowl I'll give you your hundred if you give me your wicket'. Small duly obliged, Patsy completed his century and next ball struck out, middled it even to his own astonishment and sent the ball soaring out of the ground onto the corrugated roof of a shack. Small's eyes rolled. 'Musser Hendren', he drawled, 'you say you give me your wicket. Now look what you done. Praise be to God, a man go and died in that house yesterday and you wake him up!' Patsy's reply must surely have been 'Oh dear, oh dear', for that was his stock interjection.

A kindly man to youngsters, Hendren could play every stroke in the MCC coaching manual, with the hook his favourite. Towards the end of his career, Surrey were playing at Lord's when Patsy whispered to their fast bowler, Alf Gover: 'Don't pitch them too short, Alf. I can't see 'em as I used to'. Whereupon Gover bowled a series of very rapid, short-pitched deliveries which were hooked for four after four until the Surrey captain intervened. 'But he said he didn't like them short', wailed Alf.

I was not to qualify for Middlesex until 1937, but I think I proved my readiness for first-class cricket in 1936 by scoring three centuries for MCC, 114 *v*. Surrey, putting on almost 300 with Hendren, 114 *v*. Oxford University, and 112 *v*. Kent.

The scoring of a century at Lord's is a thrill at any stage of a player's career, but especially when only a teenager. We drew good gates, especially if Surrey, Kent or Yorkshire were the visitors. We were not regaled with the hallelujah choirs that open up today when counties reach the finals of the Gillette Cup or the Benson and Hedges Cup, but those pre-war crowds were rich in character. One unforgettable spectator was 'Yorkshire Annie', whose allegiance was divided between her native Yorkshire and her adopted Middlesex. She was built like a sightscreen, less mobile and normally dressed in black, which could be disconcerting if you went out to bat on a hat-trick. She would boom oaths across Lord's, offer advice to batsmen at the quietest moments of a match, and bait umpires and officials alike with any comments that crossed her mind.

Supporters regularly wrote letters to players, discussing the finer points of a match, but one missive arrived for me after I had scored 245 against Notts in 1938 en route to 1,000 runs in May. At some stage in that innings I had hooked Harold Larwood, who was well past his prime, flat and hard to the fence.

The ball pitched inside the boundary, sweeping into A stand through the front page of *The Times* newspaper held by a spectator. Three days later I received the following letter: 'Dear Mr Edrich, I would like you to know that, if I did have to have all my teeth extracted in one go, that is the way I wanted it done. Well played, sir'.

If prizes were awarded for eccentricity, a gentleman known to us as Captain Cobb would have won by a mile. A fanatically keen Middlesex supporter, he was still playing rugby for one of the Harlequin teams at the age of sixty. He dressed in grey topper and tails for matches at Lord's and would occasionally pop his head into the players' dressing room. There appeared to be nothing amiss when he did just that during a match between Eton and Harrow. 'Come in', said a player. He did – stark naked. 'Now gentlemen, I am going to give the girls a treat', he promised.

My first season went like a dream. I scored more than 2,000 in all matches, including 1,500 for Middlesex at an average of just under 50. The wickets were excellent, quicker than today's, and rolled much more. They used massive rollers, which seemed to do a better job of compressing the square than the present-day rollers. Unfortunately my first season, at twenty-one, was Hendren's last, at forty. We shared several useful partnerships, Hendren sometimes coaching me through a sticky patch in the middle. 'Watch my feet', he would say. I wish today's Test players could see how far back and across he went to hook a ball. 'Get right back when you hook', advised Hendren. 'Give yourself room and a bit more time.' If I had illusions of grandeur they rarely blossomed in a partnership with Patsy. I was lucky to receive more than two balls an over in a long stand. 'Look, son, I'm getting the runs. You be content to watch me,' he would say before nicking a single off the last ball of the over.

Walter Robins was captain of Middlesex in my first season. He was an autocrat but an inspiring leader. I grew to like the man immensely, but in my infancy before the war I wondered at his gamesmanship. If a young opposing batsman was scoring slowly, Robbie might mutter: 'You're a driver-outer. People leave the ground when players like you are batting. Get on with it for your own sake'. I thought this was a rather harsh attitude, but I could understand the reasoning behind it.

The first season closed with my selection for an unofficial winter tour in 1937-8 to India, financed by their board of control, under the captaincy of Lord Tennyson. The captain was accompanied by his wife, an American, and a French maid, an entourage that was to be of great comfort to him when he went down with an acute bout of

dysentery. Dancing one night with Lady Tennyson, I said:
'How's his Lordship?' 'Oh, he's lost about three stone
but it won't do him any harm', she grinned.

It was the first time I had been aboard a ship, the first
time I had been overseas, the first time I had worn a dinner
jacket, the first time I had tasted the subtle flavour of
caviar. And many other firsts. Nights rolled into days.
Every other passenger seemed to be a young debutante
hoping to find an army officer as a husband on her arrival
in India. Joe Hardstaff and I scored more than 1,000 runs
each on that tour, and England won three of the five
unofficial Tests.

The tour provided an ideal preparation for the 1938
season, a remarkable summer in which Middlesex finished
second in the championship to Yorkshire, who won the
title with almost monotonous regularity in those days. I
made my England debut, playing in four Tests against the
Australians, and also scored 1,000 runs in May, a feat
accomplished by Bradman in the same month. In fact it
was thanks to the kindness of the Don that I reached the
target. Midway through the month the newspapers
suggested I stood a chance of becoming only the seventh
batsman to attain the figure. I launched myself to within
shooting distance by scoring 245 against Notts on 21, 23
and 24 May, so advancing my aggregate to 881.

But then things started to go wrong. I was out for a
duck against Worcestershire, Middlesex winning by an
innings, and I did not play again until Middlesex met the
Australians at Lord's on 28-31 May. Needing just 19, I
scored 9 in the first innings. Bradman had just achieved
the feat for the second time and, clearly feeling generous
with a draw the only possible result in a rain-interrupted
match, he declared Australia's second innings closed at
114-2. I opened with Denis Compton but as I took guard
Bradman warned: 'We're not going to give them to you,
Bill'. The elusive runs eventually came, but not without
a struggle. Denis, at the other end, helped by playing a
dead bat.

In my four Tests that season against the Aussies, I made just 67 runs for an average of less than 12. It must have been one of the worst beginnings to a Test career on record. It is easy to make excuses for failure, but I experienced a chapter of dismissals that convinced me the gremlins were nesting in my cricket bag. At Nottingham in the first Test, the England opening batsmen, Charlie Barnett and Len Hutton, both scored centuries, while I waited for my turn to bat. I had grown accustomed to opening the batting for Middlesex, so I was not used to waiting a long time for my chance to bat. Bill O'Reilly, who was the greatest legspinner of my time, was bowling, but with no respect for his reputation I drove him to the sightscreen as soon as I arrived. He bowled me his quicker ball in the next over, I misjudged the pace and rammed my bat down to keep it out of the stumps. The ball squirted onto my right boot and, such was my luck at the time, it spun off onto the wicket.

At Lord's I hooked a bouncer from Ernie McCormick like a bullet straight to Stan McCabe at mid-wicket, and in the other innings got a bottom edge onto the stumps. Three unfortunate dismissals, which went down in the record books as 'out'.

Rain destroyed the Old Trafford Test and, although I batted quite well at Leeds scoring 28 on a spinner's wicket, I had disappointed the selectors. They retained me for the fifth Test but I became one of the also-rans in a match immortalised as 'Hutton's Test'. Len scored his 364, breaking records and thrilling crowds, while I contributed 12, before providing O'Reilly with his hundredth wicket in Tests against England.

A disappointing run in international cricket continued in South Africa on the 1938-9 tour when I scored 21 runs in five Test innings. It did not take a mathematician to add together consecutive scores of 4, 10, 0, 6 and 1 and arrive at 21 miserable runs. The knives were out for my sacking but I kept my place in the side for the final Test at Durban, possibly because the captain, Walter Hammond, was using me as an all-rounder. He saw me as a 'bits and pieces' cricketer. Hammond promoted me to number 3 when England batted needing 696 in the second innings of the 'timeless' Test. His instructions were unforgettable: 'Look, you're going in 3. Get a couple of hundred and we might have a chance'. I scored 219, the finest innings of my Test career, which nearly made possible an incredible victory until rain on the tenth day and the necessity to return home conspired to interrupt us. Altogether 1,981 runs were scored before we entrained to Cape Town where the *Athlone Castle* was waiting to sail home to England.

I was named one of Wisden's 'cricketers of the year' in 1939 but the vignette which accompanied the announcement was somewhat soured by a reference to the unconvincing start I had made to my Test career. 'Edrich certainly cannot complain of lack of opportunity', declared the writer. 'No other cricketer has ever been persevered with in the face of continued non-success as a run-getter.' Of course, the old cry of 'the favoured ones of Lord's' was heard and reheard, and I confess it is doubtful whether, say, a Leicestershire player would have so long been retained. Some critics had been after my head for a long time and cartoonists were etching my demise. One cartoon showed a huge set of stumps, a tiny figure with a minute bat in front of them, a duck perched upon the bails, and a huge umpire's finger pointing skywards, above a captain stating: 'Quack, quack, the sound Edrich must hear every time he goes to the wicket', or words to that effect.

Hammond and the other players did their best to console me. Hammond, in particular, was kind, often amusing, yet always maintaining his authority over the side. We forged a strong friendship, sharing a common attitude to life. Hammond, I believe, looked upon me as a mirror of his own career, a batsman who bowled a bit and loved fielding, although I hesitate to compare my talents with those of a cricketing legend. Unfortunately Hammond's career and life came in two acts, one where he played Jekyll, and the other, involuntarily, Hyde. The pre-war version of Hammond was the dashing cavalier whose batting attained in time classic poise and the habit of long domination. The post-war model was a shadow of what had gone before, a man soured by bombs and a complicated domestic life. His problems manifested themselves on the MCC tour to Australia in 1946-7 when his batting and captaincy deteriorated beyond recognition, possibly accentuated by the acute pain he felt from fibrositis. In South Africa in 1938-9 he had been a first-rate captain, two steps ahead of our opponents.

The great players of my early cricket life did much to fashion my attitude and style. Some I would copy, others reject, but all helped to shape the young Edrich as he struggled to make his way in the world. My first god was Ernest Tyldesley, the great Lancastrian batsman, a player upon whom I based my technique. Ernest averaged 45 runs an innings during a career of twenty-seven years, and I never ceased to admire his quiet skills, most evident on unfriendly pitches.

Ken Farnes, whose career was destroyed when he became a victim of the war, was another exciting cricketer. He was the fastest bowler in England since Harold Larwood and his continued presence in the Test side after the war might have helped to quell the run-getting of Bradman and company. Farnes would now be mentioned in the same breath as the great fast bowlers of cricket history if he had possessed the killer instinct. In fact he was a gentle person, whose passions had to be roused before he could become a brutal, blunt instrument.

It was my misfortune however to meet him just after he had been omitted from the third Test against the Australians in 1938. He was livid and produced possibly the fastest spell of bowling ever seen at Lord's in the Gentlemen *v*. Players match. He became an assassin that day, unleashing one unforgettable over. His second ball to me threatened temple and life, flicking my glove and forehead en route to the wicketkeeper. Fred Price, the nightwatchman, survived only one ball, and Eddie Paynter somehow the final two deliveries. Wally Hammond, standing at slip, reckoned that over was the fastest he saw . in first-class cricket.

Mention of Fred Price reminds me of the time we were playing Yorkshire and on the point of victory, which was always something to be pleased about at a time when our old rivals were on top of the world. Yorkshire's last man was Bill Bowes. He faced Jim Sims and almost immediately got a faint touch. Fred, our wicketkeeper, roared his head off as he hurled the ball skywards in jubilation. I was at first slip and jumped forward to congratulate him on wrapping up our win. As I did so the smile suddenly left Fred's face. Instead he glared at me and spluttered: 'Well, don't just stand there, Edrich – get off my teeth!'. Unknown to me, Fred had parted company with his set and I had stamped them into the ground as I ran up to smack him on the back. Still, Fred had to agree with the general view that that was one occasion the Lord's wicket really did have a bite.

Gubby Allen taught me the importance of enjoying my cricket. I can only reinforce the tribute paid to him by Denis. I once heard him say: 'I would like to be a dictator of cricket'. If I had to choose an exact opposite to Gubby, it would be his former teammate Big Jim Smith, a larger-than-life character who dominated the dressing room at Lord's when I joined Middlesex. He was the most prodigious hitter I ever saw. The drinking bars at Lord's emptied when Jim went in to bat. He swung at everything with his right foot anchored in the crease, striking at the pitch of the ball and hitting on the up. I saw him clout Dick Pollard of Lancashire over Father Time, the ball soaring twice as high as the famous weathercock. Smith, of Wiltshire country stock, was primarily a fast bowler whose batting carried a message that tailenders would be wise to follow. His philosophy was that it was better to swing a bat for twenty minutes and get 40 than fiddle about for 6. He was only serious when the pitch was unresponsive to his bowling, a frequent occurrence at Lord's before the war. Whenever Jim bent down on the square you could bet your life he was scratching some turf out of the pitch prepared for the next match, digging his fingers into the length area and cursing: 'Think of us bowlers, Harry [White, the groundsman], for Christ's sake.'

Jim Sims was the driest wit in cricket. His classic response to a boundary off his bowling was to suggest that he was 'preparing' the unfortunate batsman for dismissal. Only once was he reduced to speechlessness, in a match at Nottingham. We had painted the town one Saturday night, winding up in the company of Arthur Carr, the Notts' captain, back at the hotel. Come Sunday and Jim's larynx had packed up. He couldn't force a word out of the front, let alone the side of his mouth. He was the same when play resumed on the Monday. He bowled like a ding-bat, taking seven wickets, but whenever he hit someone on the pads, he motioned to the rest of the side to appeal for lbw, with a great wave of the arms in the manner of a conductor lifting an orchestra.

Tom Goddard, the Gloucestershire offspinner, rivalled Jim in humour. He was the number-one appealer in the game before and after the war, bawling 'howzat' for lbw irrespective of the ball's direction, height or anything else. A beautiful bowler, he propelled the ball in a gentle curve from an enormous spinning finger shaped like a sinewy hook. 'Howzat?', yelled Tom when he struck on the pad after I had scored a century against Gloucestershire. The umpire shook his head. 'Jesus Christ,' said Tom, 'you lucky devil, Bill.' The ball had rapped me on the pad four yards up the wicket.

I admired the skill, competitiveness and courage of the Australians when I first played against them in 1938. It came as a big disappointment to discover that the public relations of the 1977 Australian touring team to England bore little comparison with the friendliness of their predecessors. Jack Fingleton, Stan McCabe and I became great friends, and I found the Don, who was considered aloof, an amiable man. He swopped his cricket flannels for the uniform of the Australian Air Force, but before he could see action he was invalided out. Later he joined the Australian Army, only to find that their stringent fitness demands precluded him from their service. So he returned to Adelaide and civilian life where he worked in his stockbroking business. We met up again in 1946-7 when MCC went down under, expecting Bradman to have announced his retirement. But there he was, named for the first Test at Brisbane. I never saw him make a poorer start to an innings. He could have been out several times early on but survived a controversial catch and went on to score 187. We all said that if Bradman had been dismissed for a couple of low scores early in that series he would probably have retired.

Stan McCabe, the 'little Napoleon', was a most likeable Aussie of the immediate pre-war era. And the 232 he scored in two hundred and fifty-five minutes at Trent Bridge in 1938 was the finest innings I saw in Test cricket. He scored all but five of the 77 runs put on for the last wicket with 'Chuck' Fleetwood-Smith, which prompted Ray Robinson, the eminent cricket journalist, to recall a conversation between England's Sydney Barnes and Sir Neville Cardus in the press box at Trent Bridge. It went: Barnes: 'The finest innings I have ever seen'. Cardus: 'Think again, you saw Trumper'. Barnes: 'I repeat, it's the greatest'. Cardus: 'I'd have liked to see you out there bowling to McCabe'. Barnes (pausing): 'I don't think *I* could have kept him quiet'.

Fleetwood-Smith was a fascinating character for different reasons. Utterly irresponsible on occasions, he was a complicated person, capable of weaving magic with his left-arm spinners. I once heard him whistle 'Pop Goes The Weasel' as he sprang in to bowl in a Test.

George Headley, described as 'the black Bradman', flashed across my early life like a shooting star. I played against him in 1939 when he toured England with the West

Indies. His performances with the bat that summer are resurrected today when Viv Richards is at the crease. I reckoned to see the ball quite early in flight but Headley was into his shots before I had considered which stroke to play. He would rock onto the back foot to a ball a little short of a length, hitting it wide of mid-on or through the covers with awesome power.

Learie Constantine was another exhilarating West Indian strokemaker. His bowling, too, could be exceptionally quick but the part of his game which intrigued me most was his fielding. He would shy at the stumps from thirty yards with his back to the wicket. Only foolhardy batsmen took singles to cover when 'Connie' was on duty. He just gets my vote as the greatest outfielder I have seen, ahead even of Clive Lloyd and Colin Bland.

These were some of the men and the moments which convinced me that cricket was the finest occupation for a man before the war.

2

The golden summer of 1947

Denis Compton

Those who dismiss some of the findings of cricket history books make the point that life is a natural progression, and therefore the deeds of today must inevitably surpass those of yesterday. I too am suspicious of some of the facts I read about Grace, Trumper, Ranji and other legendary cricketers described vividly in yellowing pages, but when I have actually participated in an episode which later assumes almost folklore proportions I become irritated if others dispute its authenticity.

Such an event happened in 1947, a summer of glorious cricket in which the shackles of wartime deprivation were cast aside and the championship was restored to the south by Middlesex for the first time since 1921. From a personal viewpoint that summer represented more than four months of sunshine and runs in which I scored eighteen centuries, eleven of them in July and August, to break Jack Hobbs' record of sixteen hundreds. I also passed Tom Hayward's record aggregate of 3,518 runs, established forty-one years earlier, to finish with 3,816. Yet, despite the runs and the records, some people remain adamant that the Compton-Edrich run spree for Middlesex and England, which earned us the title of 'the terrible twins', was largely inevitable in a summer ripe for batting.

They argue that the bowling was inferior to much that we see in England today; fielding was poor - its placing lacked imagination; and wickets of the immediate post-war era were brown havens for batsmen. I hope I shall not make the mistake of becoming equally dogmatic in arguing against these opinions, because they bear more than a grain of truth. But never was the old adage, 'seeing is believing', more appropriate than when applied to a summer in which the sun beamed from sapphire skies from June to September, spectators came to the grounds in their Morrises and Fords fuelled on rationed petrol, Christian Dior was creating an exciting range in women's fashions, and if you jogged past Lord's on match days you were likely to see Jack Robertson, Syd Brown, Bill Edrich or myself at the crease. We accumulated more than 12,000 runs between us (Compton 3,816, Edrich 3,539, Robertson 2,760, Brown 2,078), scoring thirty-three of the thirty-seven individual hundreds for Middlesex.

It is difficult to talk of that record-breaking summer in which Middlesex were undefeated in twenty-four of their thirty matches without sounding conceited and just as vehement as the detractors. But to those who live cosily in the present at the expense of the past I would suggest that of the current England side only Geoffrey Boycott of Yorkshire has the technique and application to have emulated our feats in 1947, given the same number of innings, the same bowling and the same conditions. Even then Boycott would probably not have accumulated the runs at the rate the Middlesex captain, R.W.V. Robins, demanded of us. One has to go back several seasons to find England players of sufficient talent to have challenged our records. Ignoring my contemporaries, I can think of only one other, Peter May, who might have scored eighteen centuries in fifty innings. Tom Graveney, Ted Dexter and Colin Cowdrey might have come close to succeeding but, as authoritative as they were in full flight, each lacked the consistency necessary for sustained century-making over a whole summer.

Pitches in those days were ideal for batting. The new-ball attacks of most counties did lack the initial penetration of Procter, Roberts, Willis, Hendrick and Old. Overall fielding was inferior, and so was field placing. But on the plus side, captains demanded runs at a higher rate;

the priority of batsmen was to entertain rather than remain, sometimes at the expense of their own wickets; and the battery of medium-paced bowlers and spinners we faced were accurate and controlled, capable of dictating proceedings unless a batsman took the initiative. It must also be remembered that, if records were to be broken and titles won, runs still had to be scored and, just as important, teams had to be bowled out.

To keep the two eras in perspective I concede that Barry Richards (Hampshire) and Viv Richards (Somerset), who is probably the finest batsman to have come from the West Indies, could have accomplished the same feat. I have the very greatest respect for the exciting way they get their runs, fighting for good scores against strategic field placing and defensive bowling. They are compelled to work much harder for their runs. While Derek Underwood is normally bowling to get you out, he occasionally bowls defensively, as in the Benson and Hedges final at Lord's in 1977. Alec Bedser, Cliff Gladwin, Trevor Bailey, Tom Goddard, Jim Laker and Douglas Wright were bowling at the stumps. The stroke-play in 1947 far excelled anything we have seen by an England player in recent years, even in matches against the weaker Test sides on wickets conducive to good batting.

There are several other misconceptions about 1947 I wish to clear up, for if I achieve nothing else I may persuade the sceptical that the best of thirty years ago harnessed to the best we see today might benefit future English cricket.

Records aside, the most cherished memory of that summer was clinching the championship and the manner in which we won the title.

Walter Robins, small of stature but brave of heart and conviction, led us like some crusading D'Artagnan, the like of whom I have not seen since. He would win the toss more often than not - I cannot truly claim our calling was better in those days - and Syd Brown and Jack Robertson would be searching for runs from the off. Their role was to provide a bright start, so that the rest of us could plunder freely before Robins looked for a declaration about five o'clock with more than four hundred runs on the scoreboard. He liked to be in the field for the last hour, more often than not claiming a couple of vital wickets.

Yes, ball could and did triumph over bat. Indeed, it might surprise those who believe that that summer was all runs and no results to discover that, of the four hundred and forty-two county matches played, only a hundred and twenty-two failed to produce a result. Assuming bowlers, not batsmen, are largely responsible for victories, another misconception is rolled in the dust.

Middlesex drew only two matches in the championship - another illustration of Robins' cavalier approach. His desire for results tallied with my philosophy. He would talk quietly to us before the start of play, analysing the opposition and building confidence so that by the time we went down the pavilion steps the adrenalin was fairly coursing through our bodies. Our over rate was a credit to the game. So was the run rate. If a batsman went off the boil, Robbie would get a message to the wicket, leaving the player in no doubt that he was wanted back in the dressing room sharpish if he could not raise his game.

Despite my earlier remarks about field placings, Robins was a stickler for holding catches and slick ground fielding. He set a marvellous example himself at cover point. Bill Edrich and Jack Robertson would pull off tremendous catches in the slips, and even Jack Young, never the most agile of men, would hold anything that came his way. In the outfield Jim Sims was never still, walking in yards from deep third man, fingers restless, believing that every ball would take a wicket. I could normally be found at fine leg, often in plimsolls after a good innings, relying on a strong left arm.

I scored only just over 200 runs in my first eight innings, and did not anticipate scoring more than two thousand by the end of the summer. But the match against the South Africans at the end of May raised my hopes considerably.

I made just over 150 against Alan Melville's side in the first innings of the Middlesex game, and went on during the season to score more than 1,000 runs against them, including six centuries, four in Tests.

A story in the London *Daily Express* was the first indication I had that Jack Hobbs' record, established in 1925 when he was forty-two, existed, let alone that it was threatened. Until I read that story, individual milestones had not crossed my mind. Unfortunately, the newpaper article put pressure on me to start considering my individual contribution, yet only once that summer do I recall batting selfishly, placing personal performance before that of the team. It happened in a match against Lancashire at Lord's, when I went to the wicket needing one century to equal Hobbs' record. I reached 90 fairly freely in the second innings but then took almost half an hour to achieve the target, finally sweeping Dick Pollard to the square-leg boundary to hoist my hundred. More than twenty thousand spectators rose in a memorable salute, while I pondered on the fact that the nineties are only perturbing to a batsman who is more conscious of personal performance than the fortunes of his side.

Reaching a century became an excuse that season for trying to murder the bowling. Most batsmen have experienced that wonderful feeling of wanting the next ball, and the next ball, then crashing sixes over extra cover or sweeping fours from the off stump. I was so confident after a while that I added two new shots to my repertoire. I had always loved to hit a ball on the off side, and managed to develop a cover drive which propelled the ball wide of cover point's left hand. I allowed the ball to come on a bit more than for the shot through extra, angling the bat slightly and allowing the natural left-right curve to send the ball to the boundary. The late-late cut, sometimes played between the wicketkeeper and slip, was another innovation, used mainly to score fours when my run supply to the leg and cover boundaries were cut off. The late-late cut proved most effective in a match at Lord's against Kent in which Brian Valentine's fielders were all round the boundary.

Another misconception was that I never took net practice. Archie Fowler, the Middlesex coach, gave me a ten-minute loosener before the start of play at most home matches. My whole approach to the game was geared to destroying the immaculate line and length employed by bowlers of that era. If batsmen failed to take the initiative, they were turned to stone by the accuracy of most bowlers. A shot I did not play that summer was the straight drive, although I do recall one such stroke to the sightscreen in another summer against Hampshire. Robbie, batting at the other end, had joked: 'All sorts of shots, Denis, but never the straight drive'. Vic Cannings, the Hampshire seam bowler who made me his 'rabbit' over the years, dropped the next ball perfectly - and back it went, over his head, to the rails. Robbie beamed, shaking his head, knowing it was a one-off; I used too much bottom hand to play that stroke effectively very often.

Len Hutton and I were often the subject of comparison in 1947. 'Len's a better strokemaker', the purists would say. 'Give me Compton any time for excitement', another, probably of southern origin, would argue. Our styles were remarkably different: Len's, all left-hand, my game very much right-hand even when playing shots through the covers. Len was more elegant, more disciplined, more reliable, a great player on all wickets. I could be more aggressive. If we batted together Len would applaud my 'luvely' sweep, a hook or a slashing drive past cover point, but never an orthodox stroke through mid-on, which he could play infinitely better. He respected my ability. Similarly, I loved the imperious manner in which he scored his runs. Len was the greater batsman.

Maurice Tremlett, playing his first match for Somerset, gave me more trouble than most bowlers in 1947. Tall, fairly rapid with a lovely action, he took eight wickets in Somerset's defeat of Middlesex at Lord's. He dismissed

me for 25 in the second innings, part of an inspired spell in
which he sent back five men in five overs for eight runs.
The sportsmanship was such in those days that the entire
Middlesex side lined up to applaud the victorious Somerset boys from the field. Sadly, Tremlett was never to
fulfil the rich promise of that first summer in which he
claimed more than sixty wickets. He was a failure with the
ball in South Africa in 1948-9, freezing whenever given the
responsibility of using the new ball. He bowled wides,
long-hops and half-volleys as if it were a village match. In
the end, he did not even want the new ball.

No bowler tried harder to curb our prolific run-scoring
than Tom Goddard, Gloucestershire's genial off-spinner,
who came third in the national averages with more than
two hundred and thirty wickets. He would snap his fingers
from left to right across the ball to impart tremendous
spin, and that familiar snap served as Morse code to me.
I would listen for the flick of Tom's fingers before
advancing down the wicket in an effort to defeat flight and
length. I went down the wicket to him continuously in
scoring 246 for Middlesex against the Rest at the Oval,
once tripping but hammering Tom for four as I lay prone.

'One of these bloody days, Denis, one of these days,
there will be no return ticket', he threatened. The moment
arrived in another season when he spun the ball between
bat and pad, leaving me stranded down the wicket,
stumped by four yards. Quick as a flash Tom's hand
swept into his pocket to produce a piece of paper. ''Ere
y'are, off yer go, Denis', said Tom, handing me the scrap.
I opened the crumpled slip back in the pavilion to discover
it was a bus ticket – a single fare at that.

If I put Goddard to the sword at times, Yorkshire
brought me back to earth at Headingley, where I made
just 4 and 15. We won the match but were given a fright on
a moist, sometimes spiteful wicket. Bill Edrich played one
of the finest innings of his career in our first knock,
scoring 70 out of 124 against some balls that rose
alarmingly from Alec Coxon and Bill Bowes. Jack Young

and I took four wickets apiece to limit Yorkshire; then we were treated to another magnificent innings from Bill, this time scoring 102 runs out of a total of 234. The first five deliveries from Smailes with the new ball went from his bat for 4, 6, 4, 4, 4.

I received some terrible stick from the crowd on the fine-leg boundary in that match. 'So thee is t' golden boy', they would taunt. 'Nay, our Len's t' golden boy, not thee, lad.' The Yorkies loved to see Compton failing in the north, an occurrence that was to become too regular for my liking. Len and I were seen as arch-rivals for a mythical batting crown, a rivalry created by others but never shared by the two participants.

Competition between Yorkshire and Middlesex was always something special in those days . . . and a missed catch would cause an agony of conscience. Patsy Hendren used to tell of the time some years before my debut when George Macaulay, a combative bowler for Yorkshire, watched unbelievingly as not one but three slip catches went down in his first over of the day against Middlesex at Lord's. As the third hit the ground George put hands to hips and addressed everyone in general with the words, 'Hands up those who are playing'. The affrontery of it was still rankling with George when Yorkshire returned north that night. In the train someone read out the news that Madame Tussaud's had been burned down and the owners were seeking wax figures. 'They can have my bloody slips', was Macaulay's immediate reaction.

The most remarkable match during that 1947 summer was the one at Leicester in July, a game which yielded more than 1,400 runs. Bill, leading Middlesex for the first time, recounts the match, but the game became memorable for another reason. It was the moment I learned to bowl properly.

'How do you bowl that stuff?', I had enquired of Jack Walsh, Leicestershire's left-arm spinner from Sydney, Australia. The following day he took me to the nets after breakfast to demonstrate the grip and the delivery for the left-arm wrist-spinner's chinaman and googly, adding a postscript; 'You'll get a lot of fun, Denis – but a lot of hammer, too'. The fruits of this bowling instruction blossomed at the Oval a month later when I took twelve Surrey wickets. Come the end of the season, I had taken more than fifty wickets for Middlesex.

So it was with some pleasure that I bumped into Jack Walsh in London at the end of the season. 'Enjoy it, Denis?', asked Jack. 'Great - quite a bit of success, Jack', I replied. 'Good, because I noticed you also had plenty of hammer, Denis', beamed the Australian. My wickets for Middlesex had cost twenty-five apiece.

I felt that the best innings I played in Tests was 163 in England's second innings at Trent Bridge in a match seemingly lost. Just over a hundred and fifty were required to avoid an innings defeat when Norman Yardley joined me after England had followed on. We proceeded to establish a record fifth-wicket stand of 237, leaving South Africa the task of scoring about two hundred and twenty to win in a hundred and forty minutes. Melville scored his second century of the match but his side never went for the runs and were well short at the close.

My best innings in the county games came in August against Kent at Lord's when we were set to score 397 to win at more than ninety an hour. For once, Robertson and Brown failed but I was soon into my stride, racing towards my thirteenth hundred. When play stopped for drinks, I took the opportunity to seek some tactical advice from Walter Robins standing on the balcony. 'What shall I do?', I called from below. 'What do you want to do?', he asked. 'Go for them', said I. 'Well, that's what you're going to do', said Robins. We lost by 75 runs. I reckon that innings was the finest of my career, including the 300 at Benoni for MCC against N.E. Transvaal in 1948-9.

The only bleak moment in that summer was my despair when my right knee locked while playing against Lancashire at Lord's towards the end of August. Bill Tucker, the sportsman's surgeon, discovered a piece of bone floating in my knee when he gave me a manipulative operation in the pavilion. That was the start of the knee trouble that was to plague my career and ultimately force me into retirement. It became almost as much a talking point in sport as Marlene Dietrich's legs in show business. There the comparison ends for, after three minor operations to remove pieces of bone followed by a major operation in 1956 when osteo-arthritis of the knee was diagnosed, my limb was as ugly as Miss Dietrich's were attractive.

Umpires like Frank Chester, Frank Lee and Alex Skelding contributed as much as anyone to the spirit of '47. Middlesex loved it if Skelding, then aged sixty-one, was standing. Snow-white hair under a trilby hat, glasses and big white boots beneath floppy trousers gave him a comic presence, in sharp contrast to the fear he struck into batsmen when he used the new ball for Leicestershire before and after the First World War. He would whip off the bails at the end of play with the parting words: 'That's it, gentlemen. This concludes the business of the day. Thank you'. Fifteen minutes later he would be in the Tavern at Lord's, supping a pint. He walked as briskly as Buster Keaton between square leg and the stumps, sometimes quoting Rudyard Kipling en route. But Alex reached the zenith of his poetic powers in giving young fast bowlers a rendering of 'Skelding' Shakespeare. 'Now, my boy, stiffen the sinews, summon up the blood, disguise fair nature with hard favoured rage . . . .' He would pause for a second, point at slips before pronouncing with a dramatic sweep of the hand. 'Look at them, they stand there magnificent, like greyhounds. Go to it, my boy.'

Alex was good but not the greatest umpire on account of his failing eyesight. 'Howzat, Alex?', bowlers would scream. 'No, no, no, just missing the leg stump, my boy. Worth a shout, but not owut, not owut.' Harold Butler, the Nottinghamshire pace bowler, tested Alex once when he rapped me on the pad with my leg right back in front of the stumps. Harold leapt in the air, rending the

ground with a terrible appeal. 'No, no, no, very close,
Harold, very close, just doing a bit too much.' Harold,
grinning, snapped back: 'You old so and so, Alex. I know
you like the boy, but not that much, surely?' Occasionally
an appeal would succeed, Skelding suggesting the unfortunate batsman should go to the pavilion for a little rest.
The game was the poorer for his retirement in 1958 after
twenty-seven years on the umpires' list, a reign exceeded
in length only by Frank Chester.

Harry Baldwin, who disguised his Cockney accent
behind an air of sophistication cultivated when he was
appointed to the umpires' list, was another favourite that
season. Neat and dapper, he would whisper: 'Keep it
going, Denis. It's a good wicket. No reason why you
shouldn't make another hundred today. Don't forget to
call me 'sir'. Tell Bill and the others I don't want them
calling me ' 'Arry'.' Oops, the veil had dropped a shade to
reveal his true London origins.

A silver salver, presented to me by Sir Pelham Warner
at Hastings in honour of my record-breaking seventeenth
hundred for the South against the South Africans, remains
one of my most treasured possessions. Every century was
inscribed in the silver. My wife, Christine, polishes it at
least once a week at our home in Fulmer, Bucking-
hamshire.

Another cherished moment was a dinner given in my
honour by the local authority at Hendon, my birthplace.
The town presented me with a beautiful cigarette box
which I keep filled whenever we have guests. My father,
Harry, went along that night, apparently to remind guests
that he had made my first bat when I was six and watched
my first innings in the street outside our house in
Alexandra Road, Hendon. 'There isn't a house in the
street where I haven't mended a broken window', he told
guests proudly.

My final abiding memory of 1947 was the joy it brought
to thousands of spectators. Stacks of good-luck letters
would be sent to Lord's. I must have the largest collection

of four-leafed clovers of all players. The subtle aroma of expensive French perfume would drift gently upwards when I opened some letters, occasionally to reveal a lock of hair or bequests of a more personal nature.

The fun, the runs, the gifts, the glory . . . I just wish some of the doubting Thomases had been there to see the greatest summer of my life.

Postscript by Bill Edrich

It was the occasion rather than the records that I remember most of that incredible summer. Four months in a normal lifespan of three score years and ten is a mere dot in the ocean. It is to me, unless the period just happens to embrace the months from May to September in the year 1947.

People ask, 'It was 225 you scored against Warwickshire at Birmingham, wasn't it?'. I remember that one but often settle for the safety of an evasive response on the more obscure questions. The episode has become more important to me than the statistics. I have found it increasingly difficult over the years to assess the quality of our run-getting that summer. Cricket authors and columnists have also been at variance over our contribution. That delightful essayist R.C. Robertson-Glasgow wrote:

> . . .already they are kings; benevolent kings appointed and acclaimed by like-minded subjects; champions in the fight against dullness and the commercial standard. In their cricket it is what they are that matters far more than what they have done. They stand, in these eyes at least, for something which has no place prepared in the books of score and record . . . . That such players should break records is inevitable rather than relevant.

In sharp contrast, Hubert Preston, editor of Wisden, was moved to observe:

> Frequently the bowlers were worn down before

Edrich and Compton went to the crease, whereas Hayward was number one in the Surrey batting order. Hobbs, also opening batsman, achieved his triumph under the disconcerting fire of 'another failure by Hobbs' every time he did not put up a century when approaching the 126 three-figure innings played by W.G. Grace.

More recently Colin Cowdrey, in his autobiography, wrote;

> There is no doubt that the cricket watched by the big crowds just after the war gave a false impression. They saw a run-harvest which delighted them. But I doubt if one in a hundred understood that what they were really watching was total batsman-domination of mediocre bowling . . . . As long as the runs flowed the spectators did not spend too much time making a critical analysis of the field placings. Nor did one frequently read the critics tempering their eulogies of Denis Compton's second century in a match by pointing out that the opposition bowling after the initial burst, or apart from one good spinner, was often there to be plundered.

Basically Cowdrey has always been pro-Compton but he saw fit to detract a little from his performance in 1947. Is his assessment soundly based? After all, he was only fourteen years old that summer. Trevor Bailey, who played that season and in many others and bowled to Hutton, Washbrook, May, Graveney, Barrington, Dexter, Cowdrey, Boycott and the rest of our leading batsmen since the war, has said that of all the great batsmen he bowled against, Compton, in 1947 and in other summers, was the most brilliant.

I have always doubted whether critical comparison of events and eras in sport achieves anything. It matters not, I suggest, whether Stanley Matthews was as dazzling as George Best; Montgomery the equal of Rommel; an evening of Minnelli as entertaining as a night of Garland.

More important, surely, is that they came, they performed, and when they left the stage they had thrilled. Comparisons in the context of cricket can be odious and often irrelevant. What is not in dispute is that 1947 gave more pleasure to more spectators than any other single season in cricket history. Nearly two hundred and eighty thousand watched Yorkshire at their home grounds. Kent reported record attendances of more than a hundred and eighty thousand. Lancashire's membership soared to five thousand, and Bill Bowes, my old England colleague, pocketed more than £8,000 from his benefit with Yorkshire.

Colonel R.S. Rait Kerr, secretary of MCC, was compelled to study the figures more than most when the government suggested that the pull of cricket might be interfering with industrial production in this country. At two meetings in Downing Street Rait Kerr somehow persuaded the Home Secretary that there was no such interference although, judging by some of the friends I met behind the pavilion at Lord's that summer between the hours of nine and five, he might have misjudged the situation.

Middlesex were locked in a struggle for the title while these top-level discussions were going on. We were neck and neck with Gloucestershire but victory over them at Lord's, followed by another win at Cheltenham, settled the issue.

The stage was set for a memorable summer from the moment we took the field against Somerset in May. Spectators spent their war gratuities freely at the bars, and as entertainers we responded to their enthusiasm. We felt good. Flesh had been restored to spare ribs after a measly war diet. Another stimulant to me was the freedom of playing my first season as an amateur. If I lacked much of the charisma of A.P.F. Chapman, a giant amateur of the pre-war era, I felt just as wildly enthusiastic about cricket as the former Kent and England captain. I do not propose to describe my twelve centuries that summer, including

three against the South African touring team, nor do I
intend to give a blow-by-blow account of the accumulation
of 3,539 runs to beat Tom Hayward's record aggregate,
but perhaps the reader will bear with me if I select a few
which remain etched in my memory.

The match at Leicester was memorable for two reasons –
the manner in which victory was achieved and the honour
of leading Middlesex in the absence of Walter Robins. We
had a fair old party at the end of the first day's play, a
Saturday, which illustrates our 'fun' approach to cricket
that summer. In the small hours of Sunday we wound up
the party by indulging in an impromptu game of cricket
along the corridor of the Grand Hotel, Leicester. The
Hon. Luke White - who played only twice for Middlesex
that season but came in for that match - opened the bowling.
The problem was to find a ball, a situation remedied when
I climbed out of my bedroom window, along a ledge, to
Denis's room. A few minutes later I emerged through his
door clutching a brass knob from his bed. I bowled for
hours that night, the ball keeping its shine until well after
dawn.

Then it was back to work. The match was remarkable,
from the time I won the toss on a dampish wicket to the
afternoon of the third day when we won by 10 wickets. At
lunch on the last day, Leicestershire led by 17 runs with
six second-innings wickets to fall and only an hour and
twenty minutes of the match remaining. There was no
apparent chance of victory when I asked Jim Sims to bowl.
He soon took a couple of wickets. Paddy Corrall, the
Leicestershire wicketkeeper, came in and offered a broad
defensive bat. I watched his stonewalling for a few
minutes, then said: 'Paddy, why are you playing like that?
There is no way we can win this.' The next ball he holed
out to Laurie Gray in the deep, and before we knew it
they were all out, leaving us 66 to get in twenty-five
minutes. 'Come on, Denis, we're going for them. Pad up',
I said as we hurried from the field. I posted the Middlesex
side round the boundary in case the Leicester crowd were

a bit dilatory in returning the ball, and opened myself with
Denis. Seven overs later we scored the winning run with
just four minutes to spare.

My best innings was 150-odd not out, scored against
Surrey at the Oval in August, as much a triumph over pain
as over the attack, which included Alf Gover and Alec
Bedser. I had torn shoulder muscles in striving for an
extra yard of pace against the Kent tail in the previous
match at Canterbury. The extent of that injury can be
gauged by the fact that I did not bowl another ball that
season, and apart from the Surrey match scored only one
more century, for Middlesex against the Rest, in the
remaining twenty innings of the summer.

My knock against Surrey gave me tremendous pleasure.
Bill Tucker had strapped me up, restricting my range of
shots to the minimum. My problem was that, if Alf Gover
pitched short, I was powerless to punish the ball with a
hook. His bowling partner, Alec Bedser, gave me more
trouble than any other bowler that summer. I always had
great difficulty in detecting his inswinger, or the ball that
left the bat, both deliveries apparently bowled with the
same action. So my innings consisted of prods and pushes,
sandwiched between occasional drives played mainly with
the left hand controlling the stroke.

Batting with Denis was always a great joy, never more
so than in 1947. Our leading partnerships were 370 for
England against South Africa at Lord's; 287 for Middlesex
against Surrey; 277 for Middlesex against Leicestershire;
228 for England against South Africa, at Manchester; 223
against Sussex and 211 against Northamptonshire.

We learned to raise our standards to the other's needs
and wishes. If I was bogged down, Denis would take
control. Nothing needed to be said. Our only negotiations
at the wicket seemed to be confined to making decisions
on the desirability or otherwise of taking a single to cover.
It is a myth that Denis ran badly between wickets. He
could be a fine judge of a single, erring only occasionally
by forgetting the reputation of the fielder. 'Come on', he

would say, pushing the ball to cover. 'No', I would yell
back as Cyril Washbrook or Neil Harvey closed in for the
kill. By now Denis would be nearly halfway down the
wicket shrieking, 'Oh, Christ!', before dropping his bat in
mid-pitch and making good his ground. I exercised my
prerogative in saying 'no' more than once that season.

No other county had the team spirit that we enjoyed in
1947. I should think there was hardly a shove-halfpenny
team in the country that could touch the Middlesex boys.
Jack Young struck a superb length with the coins; Harry
Sharp, Alec Thompson, Jim Sims, Denis and I were also
useful exponents. Our reputations grew on the circuit and
challenges were received from pub sides wherever we
played in the south - they do not play the game much up
north. I recall several stirring matches against a pub side
in Canterbury. I sometimes thought that our board,
polished and powdered like a baby's bottom, was nursed
with greater care than our cricket equipment. 'Where is
it?', enquired Jim Sims on one occasion just before
walking out to bat. 'In your bag, staring you in the face', I
replied, pointing to his bat. 'No, not that, Bill, the board,
the board . . . .'

Another of our pursuits was following the horses.
Copies of *Sporting Life* and *Timeform* would always have
precedence over other newspapers. Hampshire's Jim
Bailey and Len Crease were the most reliable tipsters in
the business, always good for forecasting the result of the
3.30 somewhere. Colin Ingleby-Mackenzie carried on the
tradition when he became captain of Hampshire. Quite
why Jim Bailey bothered to pass on the information to
Middlesex was a mystery, for once the match started we
would give his left-arm slows some frightful hammer. A
big, fat fellow with an immense backside and a sense of
humour to match, he would more or less walk up to the
wicket to bowl. If he was clobbered, his approach would
drop to funereal pace. Sometimes we considered placing
bets on whether the ball had enough impetus to reach the
other end.

Most days would end happily with the Middlesex team sharing a few beers in a bar. Jack Robertson, normally to be seen clutching a glass of orange juice, was a teetotaller and a non-smoker but would join in all the fun. Long days in the field followed by evenings in good company made us rest easily at night. Few of us had time to ponder on the possibilities of records even in that glorious summer.

3

Batting

Denis Compton

The prophets of doom continue to warn us that England's batting has been in steady and sad decline since the great batsmen of the classical dynasty departed the scenes of their glorious triumphs. Writers such as Neville Cardus, R.C. Robertson-Glasgow, John Arlott and Jim Swanton have perpetuated the memories of Trumper, Hobbs, Woolley, Hammond, Hendren, Hutton, May and other great batsmen so vividly that one sometimes believes that those same immortal players are still going to the wicket. One of the immense joys of following cricket is to think you actually saw Jack Hobbs score one of his hundred and ninety-seven hundreds when in reality it was achieved by sitting up in bed reading a passage from the pen of Cardus.

My only question-mark against the influence of these writers on our beliefs and attitudes is that their works have tended to obscure the fact that every generation has produced some very ordinary batsmen, some of whom on occasions have been chosen for England. One of the myths is that the technique of English batsmen today is largely inferior to that of their predecessors. We are told that if Hutton, Washbrook, Hammond, Edrich and Compton had faced Lillee and Thomson in 1974-5 England would never have lost the Ashes. Yet those players were in the England side bowled out by Miller and Toshack at Brisbane in 1946 for 141 and 172. It was not the first time we had collapsed, nor was it to be the last.

I do not subscribe to the theory that our batting is going from bad to worse. We have been shorn of some class in an era of standardisation and levelling out, in which the rich have been made poorer and the poor richer, but great batsmen are born of the womb, not of the coaching net. Sadly, the shortage of first-class batsmen at the moment has exposed the vulnerability of lesser players who have been thrust into the breach.

Poor batting at Test level is not a new phenomenon. The Australian touring team of 1977 were the worst I have ever seen wearing the baggy green cap, but Ian Johnson's 1956 side were none too good with the bat either, and nor were the Australians in 1970-1. I can recall several instances of the England selectors awarding caps to batsmen who, while admirable at county level, were never truly of Test calibre. Yet at a time when England possesses a paucity of batsmen with exceptional talent, the overall standard of batting around the counties is quite high, if not higher than in the past. I am sure, for instance, that several of the present-day lower-order batsmen from Kent and Essex would have commanded much higher batting positions in their respective counties in the immediate post-war years.

What disturbs me most is not the shortage of class at our disposal but the attitude of some of our batsmen. We have players of ability who are just not producing the performance of which they are capable. How often have television video re-runs of dismissals exposed poor appli- cation in the batting of, say, Keith Fletcher, Dennis Amiss, Derek Randall or Tony Greig when facing the very fastest bowling. Greig's choice of stroke when he comes to the wicket in a tight situation makes me wince. If Hammond was bowled by Martindale, you could bet your life that the West Indian had earned his wicket. The critics would not have pointed to a blemish in Hammond's technique in searching for a reason for his dismissal. No one deliberately throws his wicket away at Test level, but some players have given me the impression of not wanting to get their heads down when the storm has reached its full height. David Steele was acclaimed a national hero for his

plucky performances against Australia in the summer of
1975. In truth, the Northamptonshire batsman simply got
into line, living up to his name with innings founded on
determination rather than the putty-base some of his more
illustrious colleagues employed. David Steele, inci-
dentally, made his Test debut at Lord's, a ground he knew
well enough from playing there with Northamptonshire.
But he had always walked out to bat from the visitors'
dressing room. England use the home dressing room, and
when David's turn came to bat he took the wrong turning
and ended up in the lavatories! It says much for his
phlegmatic temperament that with Dennis Lillee and Jeff
Thomson bowling at their fastest he went on to complete a
splendid 50.

Not only do some of our leading batsmen become
vulnerable to pace, they have even looked frightened on
occasions. No one revels under bombardment from
bowlers capable of propelling a cricket ball at almost one
hundred mph, but I cannot recall many former England
players looking so apprehensive. Once a batsman shows
fear he is a dead duck in Test cricket. Australia's Dennis
Lillee, for one, has the stamina and the inclination to
haunt a batsman until his retirement from the Test arena if
he senses a lack of application. It would be foolish to
suggest that Bradman or McCabe did not experience fear
during the 'bodyline' onslaught from Larwood and Voce
in 1932-3, but if they were anxious for their safety they
never showed a lack of courage.

I can recall experiencing fear only once in my career. It
happened in the third Test against the Australians at
Manchester in 1948 after a ball from Lindwall flew from
my bat and struck me smack near the eyes. I went off to
hospital, returning later to bat with a plaster protecting the
wound. The dressing was like a red rag to a fighting bull.
Lindwall bowled faster than I had seen him before, clearly
determined to shatter my confidence. He achieved his
objective when I started to back away slightly. It went on
for three overs until I forced myself back into line, a

triumph of determination over inclination.

The stance alone has inspired some 'experts' to write reams, yet its function is simply to enable the batsman to stand comfortably at the crease as the bowler moves in. If batsmen want to stand chest-on, let them. If they prefer to point the left shoulder at the bowler, let them. Mine, in facing Lindwall and Miller, was pointing at mid-on, the whole object is to be relaxed.

Having said that the stance is relatively unimportant, I feel compelled to dwell a little longer on the subject if only to dissuade young players from copying the stance of two batsmen who helped restore the Ashes to England in 1977. Mike Brearley and Tony Greig stand at the crease as if a puppeteer is manipulating their bats from above. I understand that they have developed their flapping-bat technique in a effort to deal more effectively with pace bowling. My fear is that youngsters will copy the style, thus perpetuating an ugly and ill-conceived mannerism. If ever a stance encouraged a fast bowler to drill the ball through the hole, this is it. Both batsmen may argue that they are rarely bowled through the hole. My complaint is that their stance presents bowlers with a bonus, an incentive to aim at the 'funnel'. The West Indies pace attack of Roberts, Holding and Daniel rattled Greig's stumps five times in the 1976 series. Hobbs, Hammond, Hendren, Hutton, May, Cowdrey, Dexter, all great players of fast bowling, gave no such encouragement, just touching the crease with a little tap during a bowler's run-up. Greig and Brearley would be wise to stand up, stand still, and save all their movement until the bowler moves into his delivery stride.

This brings me to the most important aspect of playing fast bowling, the initial movement as the ball is about to start its journey. Players, retired first-class cricketers and coaches alike have stated categorically that the only way to play fast bowling is to move the right foot back and across the stumps. The general consensus is that this method gives a batsman more time and room to play his shot. Another school of thought suggests that batsmen should go half forward. Len Hutton always edged slightly forward against fast bowlers. Bill Edrich broke all the rules, playing the fastest bowling off the front foot. But Bill knew no fear, possessing the eyes and sharpened reflexes of a cat. I preferred to go back and across but it should be left very much to the individual.

The back-and-across technique should be examined, for in my opinion those employing it are not always playing it properly. When I moved back my right boot would rest only an inch or two from the off stump. Some batsmen are creeping back only a short distance. The coaching books confuse the issue by stating categorically that if the ball is pitched up a batsman should play forward, and if it is short a batsman should rock onto his back foot. The back-foot method, against the quicks, means that all shots are played off the back foot. Good length balls or yorkers should all be played from this position. Some coaches stipulate you should go back, then forward, if the ball is pitched well up. In my opinion the searing pace of Holding, Roberts, Thomson, Daniel and others gives a batsman no time to retreat, then attack.

One of the dangers in going back and across is to go too far over, thus exposing the leg stump. I got out on several occasions in this way, either bowled round my legs or caught on the leg side by the wicketkeeper. The chances of losing your wicket to an lbw decision are greatly increased on the back foot, but the advantages of playing fast bowling from this position do outweigh the disadvantages. Batsmen who commit themselves to the front foot are severely restricted in the range of shots they can play. Len Hutton, for instance, rarely hooked a ball because of his initial half-forward movement. Alternatively, spectators rarely saw Bradman, Hammond or myself cracking off drives off the front foot against fast bowling. We were all back-foot players, cutting, hooking, glancing and driving off the right leg.

I asked Keith Miller and Ray Lindwall at the Centenary Test which types of batsmen they preferred to bowl against. 'Give me a front-foot man unless it's Bill Edrich,' said Miller. Lindwall agreed, adding: 'You can't see their stumps when they're right back and across, and they've got much more time'.

I have the deepest respect and admiration for the plight of Dennis Amiss, who tried to change his technique to combat pace bowling. The Warwickshire batsman went back and across, but the movement was so exaggerated, so unnatural that his new method did not succeed. Here is a classic but sad case of a batsman suffering from shellshock, no longer fit for battle. Fast bowlers, Lillee in particular, exercised a frightening psychological superiority over Amiss. He became extremely twitchy, moving all over the crease. Why do our batsmen move so much before the ball is released? Head, shoulders, trunk, feet should be motionless during the bowler's run-up.

The bouncer, of all the deliveries, has given England's batsmen more trouble than any other. Once used sparingly in Test cricket, the bouncer has almost become a stock ball, to the obvious discomfort of batsmen who rarely have the opportunity to play this type of bowling in domestic cricket.

A surfeit of seam has given our batsmen little opportunity to accomplish the hook stroke, an effective antidote to the bowler with a liking for the bouncer. So why attempt a hook if the stroke is not part of a batsman's repertoire? Too many of our players, including Boycott, have lost their wickets trying to hook when they might have been better advised to sway out of the way. Our men fail to understand that it is better to concentrate on avoiding the bouncer than to play injudicious shots with little chance of punishing the bowling and every chance of getting out. I would never curb a West Indian's desire to hook, but if you cannot play the stroke do not attempt the shot.

Reg Simpson, the former Nottinghamshire and England batsman, was considered to be one of our best players of fast bowling, yet he is remembered most not for the shots

he played off Lindwall and Miller, in particular, but for
those he did not produce. Simpson was a master of dodge
and weave. It was a waste of time bowling bouncers at
him. He would move inside the line, allowing the ball to
pass harmlessly by. Simpson worked on the theory that it
was more tiring for the bowler to send down a fusillade of
bouncers than it was for him to sway out of line. I am sure
that the reason we see so many bouncers today from
Thomson, Lillee, Holding, Daniel and Roberts is that they
know English batsmen do not have the sense to ignore the
hook shot. Eighty per cent, perhaps more, of the bouncers
delivered in Test cricket are innocuous. For every
delivery that threatens life, several others soar harmlessly
over batsmen's heads. Keith Miller never bowled a very
good bouncer, especially if he had lost his temper.
Lindwall's was a different proposition, skimming at your
head with the ferocity of Ted McDonald's bouncers just
after the First World War.

If I could teach England's emergent young batsmen
anything, it would be the importance of patience. I am
remembered for putting bat to ball simply because lovers
of cricket prefer to recall the experiences they enjoyed
rather than the ones that irked them. I played some boring
innings if the occasion demanded - and I want to see
Derek Randall, in particular, eliminating some of the
strokes which contribute to his dismissals without losing
the panache that is so essential to his game and England's
future.

To another pet hate of mine, the choice of equipment to
protect life and limb from a fast bowler's fury. Protect?
Endanger, I would say. If ever a man courted a barrage of
bumpers, Mike Brearley does by his decision to wear that
helmet under his cap. But is it a dangerous argument to
question the wisdom of a man protecting his skull? Who,
for instance, will forget the words of Peter Lever after
felling Ewan Chatfield with a bouncer at Auckland in
February 1975: 'I thought I had killed him when I saw him
lying there in convulsions, with his face turning purple.'

The dialogue of a horror film.

My argument is that Chatfield was New Zealand's number 11 batsman; Brearley is an opening batsman. But he is on a loser from the start if he shows bowlers he is wary of pace, whatever motive he gives. Self-preservation is of paramount importance but surely the reflexes and eyesight of sportsmen at this level are sufficient for them to survive? If Mohammed Ali can sway inside a straight left from three feet, I am sure that Brearley can avoid a bouncer from twenty-two yards.

The new large gloves are another handicap, in my opinion, whatever their merits in protecting the hands. How is it possible to grip a cricket bat properly in a pair of boxing gloves? The great batsmen have always controlled the bat with their fingers, but such a grip is rendered almost impossible by the cumbersome gloves that some of our players are wearing. I have worn the new gloves in charity matches but could never have got on with them in first-class cricket. Fluent, wristy shots are almost impossible.

And what of the introduction of heavier bats? At the risk of sounding old-fashioned, I must also challenge the wisdom of using these outsize implements. My bats, made by Warsop, weighed 2lb. 2oz. Don Bradman and Wally Hammond chose bats weighing no more than 2lb. 4oz., manipulating them like wands to plunder the best bowling wherever they played. Choice of bat is a very personal decision but my contention is that the heavier the bat the more difficult it becomes for the strokemaker to readjust his stroke if he makes an error of judgement. A delicate flick with a 'wand' can sometimes retrieve a seemingly hopeless situation. I lost count of the number of times I whirled round to dab the ball away from the off stump after I had mucked up a stroke. I am convinced that some of our players are using bats that are much too heavy for them. The normal bat weighs between 2lb. 4½ oz. and 2lb. 5½ oz., an ounce or two heavier than mine or the Don's. The more recent range of bats brought out by some manufacturers comes in weights of between 2lb. 8oz. and 2lb. 9oz. Devotees of the larger bat claim that it is geared to meet modern demands. 'It's all middle and needs no effort', 'The ball glides off even when you don't quite middle it', are typical comments expressed to me by its supporters.

I reckon the increased weight of bats has partly contributed to our weakness in hooking. The shot demands speed of stroke and timing. How much simpler it is to swot a fly with a rolled up newspaper than with a telephone directory. The sports equipment manufacturers are having a ball, and the poor batsmen have become suckers for their propaganda. Massive bats, helmets, big gloves . . . it is rather like sending Nureyev onto the stage at Covent Garden to dance the *Nutcracker Suite* in sea-fisherman's waders.

Now to the batsmen themselves. I believe we are on the threshold of an exciting new era of English cricket in which some very fine young cricketers will emerge. But first let me consider the contribution of some of the old hands.

I did not support the recall of Geoffrey Boycott after his prolonged self-imposed exile from Test cricket. Once a soldier has quit the front line because he does not agree with the policies of his commanding officer - in this case Mike Denness - his military career is over. The analogy is appropriate to cricket. Nevertheless, Boycott did return to play a crucial part with the bat in winning the Ashes in 1977. His overall performance as a batsman, therefore, is worthy of some analysis.

Boycott has an abundance of qualities including dedication, a love of batting, a thirst for breaking records, a terror of getting out. Those strengths would be enough for most people, but, for me, Boycott will never rub shoulders with the great English batsmen of the past because he does not entertain and, even with a hundred under his belt, can be contained by good bowling. Spectators can slip away from their seats for a cup of tea without missing anything when Boycott is batting. He rarely rivets one's attention, nor does he give bowlers the stick he should when his innings is well established. Gary Sobers, Rohan Kanhai, Clyde Walcott, Everton Weekes, George Headley, Neil Harvey, Bobby Simpson, Doug Walters, Ian Chappell, Wally Hammond, Barry Richards, Viv Richards, etc. have been murderers of bowling when set. Boycott's run-flow can be curbed, a weakness which prevents him from qualifying for cricket's hall of fame.

The selectors could not have made a better choice than Mike Brearley in finding a successor to Tony Greig when his defection to Kerry Packer became known in 1977. Brearley's astute captaincy did much to restore the Ashes to England. How much longer his leadership qualities can camouflage his shortcomings with the bat is another matter. I fear it is only a question of time before Brearley's lack of technique, especially against fast bowling, costs him his England place. I do not think he has the technique to play a series of long innings in a Test match. Too often he loses his wicket in the thirties.

His dismissal in the fifth Test against Australia at the Oval in 1977 is an example of his suspect strokeplay. Jeff Thomson pitched one short, the ball flew at Brearley's heart, and he promptly fended it into short-leg's hands. A Test-class batsman would have relaxed his grip to drop the ball right at his feet. If necessary, Len Hutton's bat would act like a soggy blanket to the fiercest delivery. Bill Edrich would have employed a different tactic to the ball which deceived Brearley, shouldering his bat outside the off stump to take the ball on the body. 'Painful but effective', he tells me.

Derek Randall is very much a Test-class player, with plenty of courage and a thrilling array of strokes. Who will forget his marvellous century in the Melbourne Centenary Test? My only concern is that he could go the way of Keith Fletcher, another talented strokemaker, who seemed to seize up against the better Test bowling. Fletcher played fifty-two times for England. Yet rarely, if ever, did he produce a killer innings to win a match. Randall did not reproduce his Melbourne form against the Australians in the summer of 1977, possibly because of his ceaseless fidgeting around the crease. He seemed to be off balance when leaning into his off-side shots, and consequently his strokeplay lacked authority. The late Ron Roberts, a gifted writer and inveterate tour organiser, used to offer this advice to dilatory office boys: 'Breathe faster, sonny'. I would prescribe the opposite for Randall.

Graham Barlow, the young Middlesex batsman, fell from the selectors' favour in the England-Australia series in 1977. The opportunity for this likeable lefthander to re-establish himself might come again, but he too would be wise to work on his technique. Barlow's problem is a lack of footwork. He seems to be rooted to the crease, playing firm-footed strokes at everything. I want to see him on the move, going positively back or thrusting well forward. At the moment he stands in no-man's-land, rather like David Hookes, the young Australian who was hailed as another Neil Harvey but has yet to fulfil that reputation. The defences of both batsmen are vulnerable because of their restricted foot movements.

Bob Woolmer has shown more natural ability than most in the England team. Once given his chance in 1975, he matured remarkably. He has that unique ability to make a very quick bowler look almost military medium. His feat of deception owes everything to quickness of eye, thought, and movement.

Tony Greig's batting in Tests has been enigmatic, stirringly brilliant one moment, disappointing the next. He played like a man inspired when he tore into the Aussies' pace attack while all around him floundered in 1974-75. He has a natural aptitude, without ever convincing his detractors that his best innings are not blessed with luck. Few who saw his match-winning 103 in the second Test against India at Calcutta in 1977 would doubt Greig's ability to bat his side through a crisis, but for every sensible innings there are two or three others where impetuosity rules. And few great batsmen have come in as low as number six unless they have played for teams with exceptional performers. David Lloyd, John Edrich, Mike Denness and Colin Cowdrey were never afforded the luxury that Greig enjoyed down under in 1974-5, flailing outside the off stump to slash Thomson, Lillee and Walker high over gully or the slips.

I would also question Greig's contribution as an all-rounder. He can unveil figures that bracket him with some of the world's leading all-rounders. But can you seriously quote him in the same breath as Gary Sobers, Mushtaq Mohammad, Mike Procter, Eddie Barlow and Basil d'Oliveira? It is my submission that Greig has been an infinitely lucky cricketer, revelling in the conditions that were right for him, failing so often when they were wrong. If he fails with the bat he is excused on the grounds that number six cannot be expected to win matches when the leading batsmen are failing. Similarly, if he fails with the ball he escapes serious criticism because he is not a front-line specialist bowler and is not expected to bowl sides out. Trevor Bailey of England and Alan Davidson of Australia had no such latitude when they played for their respective countries. Failure of either with the ball was a near disaster, and if Bailey's batting was rarely fluent it was a bedrock on which England pinned their hopes in a crisis.

Sustained pressure was placed upon Greig for the first time in 1976 in the series against the West Indies. He was leading England in his first full series, determined to do well. Look at Wisden in twenty years' time, and it will reveal that the England captain came fourth in the batting averages. Not bad, you might think. Examine the series a little closer. Nearly two hundred of his aggregate of 243 for the series came in the Headingley Test. Scores of 0, 6, 20, 9, 3, 12 and 1 tell the rest of the story.

I assess the contribution of our leading players by the way they play county cricket. Boycott nearly always tops the Yorkshire batting; John Edrich heads Surrey's list;

Woolmer does well for Kent. Greig's performance for
Sussex? He was seventh in their batting in 1976 with an
average of 22 and did little better the following season.
Fortunately, the influence of Packer may clear a path for
some real thoroughbreds to forge their way in the game. I
doubt whether it will be long before English spectators are
thrilling to the contributions of David Gower (Leicestershire), Chris Tavare (Kent), Bill Athey and Jim Love
(Yorkshire), Matthew Fosh (Essex) and David Rock
(Hampshire). Michael Gatting (Middlesex) and Ian
Botham (Somerset) are already becoming established and,
although I am not suggesting they will all make the top, I
have not seen a more worthy group of youngsters in the
wings for a long time.

The influence of one-day cricket has been blamed for
the deterioration of our batting at Test level. But here is a
group who are cutting their teeth on Benson and Hedges,
John Player and Gillette competitions. I disagree with the
theory that batsmen are compelled to score runs in a
restricted time and thus forced to make shots they might
not otherwise have attempted. It is true that batsmen have
to attack much earlier than they would in a Test match,
but I believe the instant game has made better players of
rather limited cricketers. Brian Luckhurst of Kent rose to
Test level on the strength of his progress in one-day
cricket.

After England's thrashing in Australia in 1974-5, Alec
Bedser, chairman of the selectors, was quoted as saying:
'Limited-over matches are no preparation for Tests.
Batsmen cannot build an innings. They are not con-
ditioned to combat an attacking opposition'. Rather than
curbing strokemaking, I believe the one-day competitions
encourage shots. The John Player Sunday cricket is a
marvellous stage for experiment. If a batsman is trying to
perfect a shot in the nets, there is no reason why he should
not use the Sunday game to air it publicly. The tight
bowling and clever field settings of the one-day game can
also serve as good preparations for Test cricket. A

batsman who can crack a defensive cordon by finding the gaps on Sundays is going to make many more runs at Test level than the player who cover-drives beautifully, but straight to fielders.

Yet if one-day cricket has been a boon to the game both economically and for playing reasons, the influx of overseas players in the past decade has had a major bearing on the shortage of native talent. The domination of overseas players has given them a stranglehold on the key batting positions in most counties. What hope has a twenty-year-old batsman from Cheltenham of winning selection in a Gloucestershire side containing Sadiq, Zaheer and Procter? I am not suggesting counties are turning away youngsters, but if Rohan Kanhai occupies a key position in Warwickshire's batting order for a decade it must surely limit the chances of homegrown players.

I applaud the Test and County Cricket Board's decision to limit counties to two specially registered players. I hope that by 1980 they will have been phased out altogether. I am convinced that spectators would rather watch a hundred from the bat of a home-developed player than one from an imported star. The overseas players never brought in the crowds the administrators expected at the outset. Even the presence of the mighty Gary Sobers with Nottinghamshire rarely filled Trent Bridge. Clive Lloyd at Lancashire, Viv Richards at Somerset, and Barry Richards and Gordon Greenidge at Hampshire certainly add spectators to the gate, but they are rare exceptions.

I feared that Yorkshire had buried their head in the sand by refusing to engage overseas players. But their rejection of the opportunity to go 'open' is now paying handsome dividends after several lean playing years. The names of Bill Athey, Phil Carrick, David Bairstow, Kevin Sharp and Graham Stevenson, all potentially gifted players, testify to the success of Yorkshire's policy. They have learned their cricket from playing, not by watching overseas stars from the sidelines. It will always be more stimulating to bite on an English tomato from the back garden than one flown in from abroad.

My only hope is that when the rich vein of talent which now runs through our cricket begins to bear fruit we will give it time to mature. Too often our selectors have discarded players after one or two bad performances with the bat. Frank Hayes, Lancashire's new captain, was one who would have benefited from an extended trial. He played nine Tests between 1973 and 1976 when the rest of England's batting was sketchy, to say the least. He made a century against the West Indies on his Test debut, failed on MCC's tour to the West Indies in 1973-4, and has never been given the opportunity his talents deserve. Bill Edrich might have played fewer than thirty-nine Tests if the England selectors had not displayed infinite patience.

Test selection is all a matter of judgement. Mistakes will be made as long as cricket is played. Fortunately our selectors may soon be placed in the enviable position of choosing from an abundance of riches, if the wind of change that I detect continues to blow in the right direction.

4

Touring

Denis Compton

The process of selecting, packaging and despatching a cricket tour party overseas has been sharpened to a level of near-perfection by the Test and County Cricket Board. Time and distance have been shrunk by the jet age. Accommodation offered by the major hotels in most of the world's important cities has become a sophisticated home from home, and if some of the food is not always agreeable to an Englishman's stomach, most of the dishes served are palatable.

A serious injury to a player, once a major emergency prompting a flurry of cables from tour base to Lord's, is now a setback of minor proportions. Colin Cowdrey was shaving at his home in Limpsfield one cold Saturday morning in midwinter and forty-eight hours later unpacking the same shaving tackle, still moist, in Perth, Western Australia after acknowledging a distress call to join MCC in 1974-5.

Yet in spite of an immense improvement in planning and operating highly complicated tour schedules hundreds of miles from home, one vital aspect of touring continues to be left largely to chance. I am referring to tour management. In six major tours overseas to Australia and New Zealand, South Africa and the West Indies, I never once felt entirely satisfied with the choice of manager. That is not to say I brushed with authority from the time we left until our return, but the tours offered moments of disenchantment when I saw the most conscientious manager fumbling to win friends at a reception, or the most charming and distinguished of tour leaders making friends with everyone he met, yet remaining dilatory on other important matters.

Disciplinarians were marvellous at imposing rules but often lacked tact, sensitivity and a ready ear for the tourists with a personal problem. Similarly, those who sympathised with the pain in your knee would probably neglect a problem of much greater importance to the welfare of the tour party as a whole.

It has long been my belief that the TCCB should inject some permanency into the job by appointing a full-time manager on a lucrative contract, say of three to five years. The supremo would be responsible for all the duties currently undertaken by the part-timers, but would provide a refreshing feel of continuity to the post in much the same way as a football manager in preparing his national side for the next World Cup. At the moment there is no guarantee that, if a cricket tour to the West Indies has been successful, the next, to India, will be run with equal efficiency under a new man. A permanent appointment made with the utmost care would reduce, if not entirely eliminate, the risks.

It would be important for a full-time overlord to have played the game at an advanced level and to have had some experience as an adminstrator. Ken Barrington is rich in these qualifications. He can draw on his experience as a tour manager and England selector and on a wealth of knowledge gained from representing his country in more than eighty Tests, many overseas. A full-time manager would take charge of England both at home and abroad, although his responsibilities here would need to be reduced considerably if the job was to be acceptable to most candidates. No man, however talented, could be expected to undertake a long winter tour, then desert his wife and family again for most of the summer. His role in England could be confined to assisting selection and generally lending a hand in supervising the smooth running of the series.

Candidates who come immediately to mind are Barrington himself, whose business interests would probably preclude him from applying, and Ray Illingworth, whose long and distinguished playing career will soon be drawing to a close. Wise, well liked, vastly experienced and a methodical and diligent professional, Illingworth has qualifications that make him eminently suitable for such an appointment. In a career embracing sixty-one Tests between 1958 and 1973, captaining England in half of the matches, he toured the West Indies, Australia and New Zealand, restoring the Ashes to the homeland in 1970-1. He helped Yorkshire win seven county championships, has led Leicestershire superbly since 1969 and is due to become team manager of Yorkshire in 1979. What pleases me most about Illingworth is his desire to accept change if it is to benefit the game as a whole.

A player's man is a necessity on a long overseas tour. David Brown, the Warwickshire pace bowler, fits this category. He is an experienced England player abroad, having made tours to South Africa in 1964-5, Australia and New Zealand in 1965-6, Pakistan in 1966-7 as vice-captain, the West Indies in 1967-8, and Ceylon and Pakistan in 1968-9. Brown is intelligent and responsible, with that rare quality of being able to command respect without appearing to impose his authority.

I would also include Jack Bannister, secretary of the Cricketers' Association, in my line-up. He is a fine ambassador for cricket, scrupulously fair, and quite capable of toeing the official line if necessary or bending a little to try something unorthodox if the occasion warrants a different approach.

And what about Peter Richardson, the former Kent and England lefthanded opening batsman? Possibly not everyone's choice, but an obvious candidate for me. His bubbling sense of fun sometimes led him into trouble with authority, but he possessed that rare ability to adopt the right attitude at the right moment - a devilish Eric Morecambe one moment, an almost Boycottian character the next. He was never more disciplined than in batting for nearly five hundred minutes against South Africa in the first Test of the 1956-7 tour.

Barrington and the Duke of Norfolk, who led MCC to Australia in 1962-3, have been two of the best men we have sent overseas. Not that Barrington has ever been allowed to forget a particular night on that tour. The Duke slept badly and during one of the Test matches he decided to take a sleeping tablet so that he would be assured of a full night's rest. He had just settled into a deep sleep when he was startled by the shrill ringing of his bedside telephone. The caller was Barrington who enquired if he might have one of the Duke's sleeping pills. He was told to hurry along to collect it. But on putting down the phone Barrington promptly fell asleep. Meanwhile along the corridor a now wide-awake Earl Marshal of England paced his room in mounting irritation. Finally he retired to bed but not to sleep. When the two met the next morning Barrington received a short, sharp lecture on the perils of forgetfulness!

To another aspect of touring, the thorniest of all - the duration of tours. It is a subject the authorities are rightly examining. Air travel has shortened trips considerably since my day, but even now players are often taken away from their homes and families from October to April. I would advocate tours of no more than three and a half months, possibly less, which could be accomplished by a sharp, but not too severe, pruning of itineraries. MCC continue to make long, arduous journeys into remote parts of some of the countries they visit, just to fly the flag. It is argued that some minor games are important in preparing for a Test series. I accept that match practice is vital, especially against the old enemy, Australia, but my solution to that would be to scrap the minor fixtures in Australia and start the tour in New Zealand. A vibrant England, thirsting for action, would be much more acceptable to the New Zealand authorities and their spectactors than the cus-tomary arrival of a wearied group of players who will have played eight Tests in less than four months by the end of the New Zealand leg. Warm-up Tests against New Zealand, followed by a few state games in Australia, would be ideal preparation for the first Test at Brisbane.

Shorter tours would also solve the question of whether wives should tour, a subject that is debated by players in hotel lounges across the world, cricket administrators at Lord's and the ladies themselves. It is an argument that is impossible to resolve satisfactorily, although I do believe that shorter tours and no wives would be the wisest decision to take. The TCCB ruling at the time of writing is that wives can accompany husbands but must find alternative accommodation. This ruling is relaxed for twenty-one days in which they are allowed to stay with their husbands in the team's hotel. This kind of arrangement can lead to unhappiness. The single members complain that they rarely see their married colleagues at the close of play and less wealthy husbands regret that their wives cannot accompany them for economic reasons.

Tony Greig revealed to the Kerry Packer High Court in London at the end of the 1977 season that Alan Knott was close to quitting over the tour arrangements for wives in India. Greig has also admitted to a charade on the MCC tour to Australia in 1974-5, when he slipped unseen at night from the team's hotel to his wife's hotel nearby, returning before morning-call the following day. I do not condone his behaviour but my sympathies are with Greig.

Shorter tours would also eliminate homesickness. Geoff Arnold, then a Surrey seam bowler, was unhappy on MCC's tour to the West Indies in 1973-4. He perked up when his wife arrived but I am sure he would have been more unhappy on the much longer trip down under. No player could have had a more understandable excuse for homesickness than Reg Simpson, the former Nottinghamshire and England opening batsman. He left his bride on the quayside only a week or two after they were married. Not surprisingly his form suffered on the MCC tour to South Africa in 1948-9 and he often expressed the opinion to me that he had given his wife an awful deal.

One of the more disturbing products of the 'free' society is the effect it has had on cricket tours. Some tour players lack the social graces of their predecessors and I see clear signs of the social side of touring diminishing in some quarters. I was disappointed with the Australian team to England in 1977. My fears were aroused from the moment they stepped off the plane at Heathrow, looking more like a working men's club returning from a weekend jaunt to Majorca than an international cricket team. Their turn-out at the Waldorf Hotel, the team's London headquarters, was just as relaxed, consisting of open-necked shirts and a motley assortment of denims. Very casual dress seems to have proliferated since the start of the Chappell dynasty. Fortunately the Australian Board of Control can take heart from the attitude of their under-nineteen team which also visited England in 1977. They restored the balance commendably by looking smart whenever they appeared in public. Mike Brearley is possibly the least conservative dresser of all England captains in history, but he seems to have struck a happy medium between Savile Row formal and Carnaby casual.

I must also take the last Australian team to task for making fewer friends in 1977 than Ray Lindwall and Keith Miller achieved by themselves in 1948. Some of Bradman's side are still exchanging letters with people they met in Yorkshire, Glamorgan, Warwickshire and other parts of England. Many of Greg Chappell's side seemed happier in their own company.

Their predecessors ran a sort of 'hearts and minds' operation as a matter of policy. I had not set foot on Australian soil in 1946 before a newspaperman came aboard the ship at Fremantle to probe me with a series of questions including: 'Any hobbies?'. I said the first thing that came into my head, blurting out: 'I love bowls'. The following day the reporter revealed to the world that Compton was a bowls fanatic. Little did he realise I had never played the game. Dozens of invitations to play the game arrived, one of which I accepted. I suppose it took my hosts less than the time it takes to drink a pint of beer to expose my ignorance of bowls. 'No Sir,' said the club official, 'woods have a natural bias, you don't have to use wrist spin.'

My bowls career, interspersed with my golf, gathered momentum on three tours in such cities as Perth, Sydney Melbourne, Adelaide and Brisbane. If I had not played golf in South Africa I would not have partnered Harold Henning. Similarly, if I had not played rounds in Australia I would never have become close friends with Peter Thomson, one of Australia's finest golfers. Making friends will always be the most rewarding spin-off of playing sport overseas and the Australian cricketers today would be wise to take advantage of the opportunities that travel offers them.

I have never fully understood the reluctance of Lord's to invite the chairman of the selectors to accompany tours abroad. Alec Bedser has spent many hours with his panel of selectors choosing the right men to fly off and then waved them farewell from the tarmac at Heathrow. The result of this stay-at-home policy is to create a situation whereby Bedser, one of the world's foremost administrators, has little first-hand knowledge of pitch conditions and climate in some of the Test-playing countries. Bedser had experience of only Australia, New Zealand and South Africa as a Test player, so how can he feel confident in choosing the right bowlers for Indian or Pakistani pitch conditions? First-hand knowledge is not always necessary in planning an operation, but a mountaineer would be unwise to lead an assault on Everest with no experience of conditions in Nepal. The chairman should be asked to accompany all-England parties with one, possibly two, of his co-selectors joining him at a later date. That way they will develop an understanding of conditions that will benefit all future trips. I would find it difficult to accept the excuse that Bedser was not invited because of economic reasons. MCC tours generally have been very lucrative.

The time is also ripe for the International Cricket
Conference to overlord the worldwide network of touring by
member countries. The system is currently haphazard with
the respective boards of control responsible for conducting
their own affairs. Tours should come completely under the
umbrella of the ICC, who should supervise with power to
eradicate faults in the system.

For example, what efforts have been made to ensure
that the internal travel arrangements in India are improved
before the next visit by England or any other country?
Transportation within the country was often very bad on
the MCC tour there in 1976-7. Greig's team were kept
waiting at airports for as long as nine hours on several
occasions. And will the England team ever forget that
Boxing Day? While most of us slept off the effects of
turkey and Christmas pudding, our cricketers were holed
up at Calcutta Airport from 7.30 a.m. until mid-afternoon,
awaiting a flight out. On another occasion they twiddled
their thumbs in intense heat for eight hours at Bombay en
route to Jaipur.

At one hotel some of the players ran a contest to see
who could kill most cockroaches. A prize was never
awarded, simply because they lost count. The floor of the
dining room was caked in thick grease. But the sub-
standard accommodation at that particular hotel created
some humorous moments, such as the occasion on which
Tony Greig entered the kitchen to discover the where-
abouts of the breakfast he had ordered some forty minutes
earlier. No sooner had he put his head through the door
than he was sliding across the floor on a skid-pan of
cooking oil. Tighter controls and closer supervision, with
the ICC circulating reports of conditions all over the world,
would help eliminate many of the problems and make life
for cricketers overseas more bearable.

It is not widely known that I came close to winning
selection for Gubby Allen's tour to Australia in 1936-7
after just one season of first-class cricket. Gubby has been
forthright enough to confess that his casting vote alone

cost me a place on the ship. He voted against me because I was too young - only eighteen and inexperienced, although he said he wished in later years he had taken a chance in giving me the last place. Stan Worthington of Derbyshire received that honour - and I waited another ten years before making the tour.

The 1946-7 tour to Australia was the most rewarding of the three tours I made down under. The joy of donning flannels abroad after a war in khaki was marvellous. The food was superb and the hospitality magnificent. Indeed our one major disappointment was the loss of the rubber 3-0, with two Tests drawn. Our bowling limitations were such that we had little hope from the outset of defeating Bradman's side. Norman Yardley was the most successful bowler in Tests, yet his ten wickets cost 37 runs apiece. Doug Wright took 23 wickets in the series, but each one cost him 43 runs.

It has remained my contention that the controversial umpiring incident in the first Test, which allowed Bradman to remain at the wicket after he was 'caught' by John Ikin at gully off Bill Voce for 28, had a greater bearing on the series than we at first thought. Bradman went on to make 187. His batting dominated the rest of the series. Hammond never forgave Bradman for not 'walking'. Indeed, his bitterness over that incident affected his judgement and attitude for the rest of the series. The two captains never dined together, Hammond confining his remarks to two words only, 'heads' or 'tails', whenever they were forced to meet face to face to toss a coin.

Hammond disappointed me. He had been an inspiring captain before the war but now we experienced aloofness in his manner, and his tactics on the field were largely defensive. He suffered from fibrositis, and he hardly had a lethal battery of bowlers to control, but nevertheless he showed a safety-first attitude that concerned us all. This was never more acute than on the morning of the second Test at Sydney. He took me aside to issue some explicit instructions on batting: 'Don't go up the wicket. Give

nothing away. Don't take chances. Wear them down'. The
tactics were foreign to my nature, but who was I to argue
with a man of such experience? I duly remained rooted to
the crease and allowed Australia's legspinner, Colin
McCool, to send us reeling on a beautiful wicket. He
picked up eight wickets, including mine for five, in the
first innings. I rarely sought Hammond's advice after that.

Bradman outfoxed Hammond in all departments. I
remember being put on to bowl when Bradman was
approaching 200 in the second Test. 'I'm packing the off
side. It's your job to bowl to the field and tie him down',
said Hammond. I bowled a perfect length on a perfect line
just outside the off peg - and was treated to some perfect
footwork by the Don, who calmly skipped across the
wicket to hit me freely to the unguarded on side.

I shall cherish my first sight of Ray Lindwall and Keith
Miller bowling in harness with the new ball. Is anything
more thrilling than the birth of a fast-bowling partnership?
I had seen Miller in the war but now he had a partner, an
athletic young bowler with a superb action from New
South Wales. The contrast in styles was staggering;
Miller, moody, unpredictable, releasing a fiendish bumper
one moment, a curving googly the next. His overs rarely
seemed to take longer than two or three minutes as he
swept in off twelve paces or cut his run-up without
warning to bowl an offspinner or googly. His spinner
would drop on a length and he would laugh his head off.
That can be disconcerting in the fourth over of a Test
match!

Lindwall was beautifully controlled, with a bouncer
eminently more dangerous than Miller's that would skim
from the pitch straight at batsmen's throats. Lindwall was
the greater of the two, yet, paradoxically, I preferred
facing him to Miller, a preference shared by Len Hutton.
Lindwall rarely, if ever, bowled a bad ball. Every ball had
to be played and watched right onto the bat. Miller could
be positively docile one moment, lulling batsmen into false
security before releasing the virtually unplayable delivery.

If ever I relaxed, Miller would send down a wicked, swinging yorker, delivered without warning but followed by a roar of laughter from the big man, especially if it happened to send the middle stump cartwheeling from the turf.

Their characters contrasted as well. Lindwall was quieter, thoughtful, a thoroughly nice person. Miller was flamboyant, unpredictable, a law unto himself. If he had a late night on the beer, England's batsmen would fear the worst the next morning. Almost invariably Keith was at his most dangerous with a headache, unleashing bumpers and the rest of his repertoire until the pain had subsided. His pace for five overs of the first innings of the Lord's Test of 1953 against Len Hutton and me was the fastest I saw in my career. I rate him second only to Sobers as the greatest all-rounder.

I developed a friendship with Miller on the first tour that flourished throughout our careers. It was based on a common love of horse-racing. We would back a horse or two every day, taking it in turns to follow the fortunes of our runners by developing a series of hand signals. If Miller was fielding, I would give him a thumbs-up or down from the pavilion once the race was decided. If we were both on the field Miller would arrange a runner to bring news to the boundary edge. A win at 10-1 inevitably led to Miller bowling me a bouncer next ball.

The most memorable Test in the 1946-7 series was the fourth, at Adelaide. I scored a century in each innings - the second, an unbeaten 103, something of a match-saving performance with a passive Godfrey Evans. Australia led by 27. We collapsed in the second innings to 255-8 when Evans joined me and proceeded to present a bat as wide as a Roman's shield. I stole the bowling at every opportunity but Godfrey was compelled to face 98 balls off which he scored precisely 10 not out.

It was during our long rearguard partnership that Bradman revealed a professional streak I accepted but did not admire. He spread his field, encouraging me to run twos and lose strike towards the end of the overs. I would have none of it, hitting freely to his men but taking only singles. 'Why don't you run? That's not the way to play cricket', he said. 'You set a proper field and I will', I replied. Then he tried a new ploy, complaining about the scuff marks my spikes were making on the pitch whenever I ventured down the wicket to Colin McCool. 'Cut it out, Denis, you're ruining the surface', he complained. 'We've got to bat after you.' 'Do you want me to take my boots off, Don?', I asked. He was not amused. Nor was Miller, who slipped me a beamer that went searing past my head for four byes. I did not see the ball from the moment it left his hand. It was the first and last time I faced a beamer. Miller's reaction? 'Denis, you were beginning to bore me playing like that.'

England's success in winning two Tests and remaining unbeaten on the 1948-9 tour to South Africa was seen as a major breakthrough to full recovery after the war. We still lacked bowlers of genuine pace, but Cliff Gladwin and Alec Bedser with the new ball and Roly Jenkins and Doug Wright with their legspin were too much for the South Africans. My most treasured memory of that trip was the 300 not out of 399 I scored in a hundred and eight-one minutes against N.E. Transvaal at Benoni. It was possibly the most unlikely innings of all time. After scoring the first century in sixty-six minutes, I was prepared to lose my wicket. But the more I swung, the greater my success. In the end I was walking down the wicket before the ball had left the bowler's hands, caring little for safety and fully expecting to get out. I hammered balls from outside the off stump to leg, stepped away to square leg to cut balls from the leg stump - did everything wrong, yet everything right.

The previous game, against Natal, had been more demanding. A nineteen-year-old fast bowler took five of our wickets in the first innings, which is hardly surprising because he was to bother the best batsmen in the world over the next few years.

He delivered his thunderbolts just as fast as Lindwall and

One of the immense joys . . . to think you actually saw Jack Hobbs batting

'I recall experiencing fear only once . . .' Compton, after being struck by Lindwall, Old Trafford, 1948

The unique
talents of Gary
Sobers

Enormous presence, aggression and speed – that was Freddie Trueman

Alec Bedser 'never gave less than one-hundred-per-cent effort'

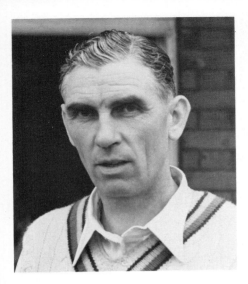

Jim Sims was always 'preparing' a batsman's dismissal

Below left: Frank Chester, shrewd, fair and incredibly courageous

Below right: Patsy Hendren, a kindly man to youngsters

Some called Don Bradman a 'run machine' but he was never boring

Eddie Paynter – 'the fun and comradeship' – in striking pose

Elegance and authority – the hallmarks of Len Hutton's batting

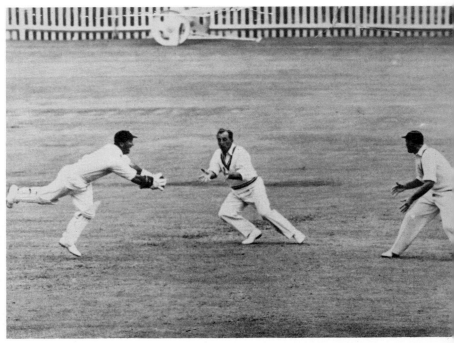

The acrobatic catching skill of Godfrey Evans

eoff Boycott *caps* his Test recall – with a hundredth 100 – but does his batting *entertain?*

Colin Cowdrey, commanding stroke maker and astute captain, says Edrich

'You'll get a lot of fun from bowling – and hammer, too!' was Jack Walsh's advice

The fun, the runs – cherished memories (Compton batting)

Down they
go! Friends
and rivals
Edrich and
Keith Miller

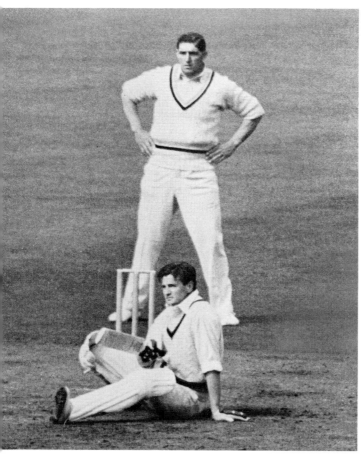

'Tich' Freeman,
a craftsman
among
leg-spinners

Norman Yardley
tosses with The
Don, his 'rabbit'
in three successive
innings

Walter Hammond, an athletic figure of high skills

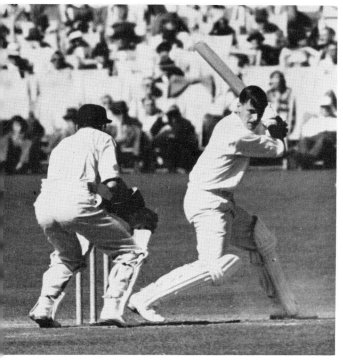

Peter May: a tragedy that ill-health curbed his Test career

Cause of all the trouble on the 'bodyline' tour – Harold Larwood bowling to his legside field

Positive, entertaining play is what the public want

Miller but with an awkward, deceptive action. It was some time before the cricket authorities had the strength of character to outlaw the bowling of Cuan McCarthy, a thrower.

By the time we played Rhodesia at Bulawayo I cared little where I rested my head. We had been on tour for four months and sleep came easily at night in the lavishly furnished and appointed Victoria Falls Hotel which offered breathtaking views of rain forests. The hotel manager approached me one morning on my way to breakfast. 'What do you think of your room, Mr Compton?', he asked. 'Magnificent, marvellous', I replied. 'It should be, sir, because the bed you're in was the one occupied by Princess Elizabeth on her tour'.

If you walk through Chesterfield, Derbyshire, today you are likely to come across a sports shop run by Cliff Gladwin. Venture inside and ask him to show you 'the trousers'. Upon close examination you will notice a mark or two, especially one around the thigh area. Take note, for those trousers have not been washed since 20 December 1948. They were worn by Gladwin when he featured in the most thrilling end to a Test I can remember. With three balls of the first Test left at Durban, any one of four results was possible. Before Alec Bedser brought the scores level with a single off the sixth delivery of Tuckett's last over, a draw or a tie could be visualised as easily as victory for either side. Gladwin swung at but missed the seventh, so both batsmen decided to run on the final ball, whatever the outcome. Gladwin heaved again as fielders hurtled in from all sides, the ball struck his thigh, and they galloped the winning single. Dudley Nourse, South Africa's captain, blundered by not telling his wicketkeeper to stand up, for had he been close to the stumps he could have run Bedser out so easily. One of the marks on Gladwin's trousers was made by that final ball.

Eric Rowan was the most fascinating character in that South African side. A man of changing moods, he scored about 30 in his first three Test innings on that tour and knew he was for the chop unless he made some runs in the second innings of the Test at Johannesburg. To our astonishment, he emerged from the pavilion without batting gloves, whispering to me as he passed by: 'I'll show them'. He scored an undefeated 156 to save the match but the runs had come too late to save him from being omitted from the next Test. Rowan seemed to make enemies as others do friends. Stories would appear in the newspapers out there quoting Rowan as suggesting that South African selectors had 'no bloody brains' and should resign on the spot.

The bubble burst on my career on my third tour in 1950-1 to Australia and New Zealand. Sadly, the eclipse of Compton's batting in that series remains a subject for debate three decades later. The Test figures tell most of the story - 3, 0, 0, 23, 5, 0, 11 and 11 not out, aggregate 53, average 7.57. Not pretty reading and utterly demoralising to someone who had tasted perhaps more than his fair share of success before. In the end we lost the series 4-1 simply because we could not score runs, with Compton the main culprit. Only once did we score more than three hundred, and had it not been for Len Hutton's masterful batting and that of Reg Simpson on occasions, we would have been beaten out of sight, despite fine bowling from Alec Bedser, Freddie Brown and Trevor Bailey.

By the time the fourth Test at Adelaide arrived even several of the Aussies were wishing me luck. I went for five in the first innings and so you can imagine how I felt when I walked out for my second knock. But as I walked past Bill Johnston, a great pal of mine, he whispered: 'You poor old cobber.... I'll give you one to get off the mark'. He was as good as his word. Down came a rank long-hop. I middled it perfectly but the ball flew straight into the hands of Sam Loxton at midwicket - and he was only the substitute fielder! That was the first and last time in my career that I was given 'a free ball'.

I became so concerned at the poverty of my run-

getting that I went to the Don for some advice. 'I feel as
if I'm batting with a stump', I said, whereupon the great
man produced a bat from beneath a bed in his hotel room
at Melbourne and proceeded to give me a ten-minute
display of magic strokes and footwork with an imaginary
ball. He reckoned I was playing across the line, was not
using my feet properly, and had lost confidence.

Some of the press gave me a hammering. One writer
went so far as to suggest that I was not conducting myself
properly off the field. His campaign reached a climax just
before the third Test, at Sydney, when I had the
misfortune to slip and cut my eye on a garden tap during a
party given by Bill Gluth, a prominent golfer, who was a
great friend of MCC. The wound stretched across the top of
my eye. It was so bad a doctor was summoned to the
party to stitch it. The injury prevented me from flying to
Sydney with the main party, and when I eventually
stepped off the aircraft photographers closed in to focus
on the eye which had now turned vermilion. I had not
shaved for two days, so the shot provided an X-certificate
horror picture for the *Sydney Sun*, which they splashed
right across their front page. In retrospect, the crisis I
experienced on that tour helped my career. I had tasted
terrible failure after so much success, the greatest ego-
deflator of all to a Test cricketer.

I believe the selectors were right to include Brian Close
in the team, despite all the criticism they faced when he
failed to fulfil his promise. He was only nineteen and was
never given the guidance one felt he should have received.
My abiding memory is of 'Closey' trying and failing so
often to sweep balls from the middle and leg stumps to fine
leg. I am sure he played many good strokes but the
rashness of those shots remains in the mind. A player is
never too young to be given a Test chance. If he is good
enough he will make the grade.

Godfrey Evans' wicketkeeping for England on that tour
is another memory I shall cherish. He was incredible from
first to last, never missing a chance in five Tests. He held

Neil Harvey from a perfect leg glance in the first Test, clutching a ball that would have gone well wide of me at leg slip. Godfrey was the best morale-booster I met in cricket, egging on his teammates as the sun sank behind the pavilion towards the end of the day. 'Come on, we've got 'em', he would shout even in the first overs of a bad day for England. Or we would emerge from the pavilion after lunch with Godfrey announcing: 'Only one wicket before lunch, let's make it five by tea'.

Evans' lifestyle contrasted sharply with that of Alan Knott, who eventually succeeded him in the Kent and England sides. Knott is well known for his fitness routines, but what is not generally known is that Evans took just as much care of his body by adopting a different method of training. Knott would be bending and flexing his muscles in his hotel room long before the start of a day's play. Evans' routine on a non-match day could be just as demanding, starting with an early morning session on the squash court, then a round of golf in the afternoon, culminating in a game of tennis in the early evening. He would then decide to round off the day by taking a Turkish bath. Who could blame the man for having a beer or two after that?

Both served England with distinction but I would choose Evans as the better wicketkeeper, simply on account of the greater variety of bowling he faced with the gloves. Alec Bedser would bend one past the bat for the ball to fairly melt into Evans' gloves above the off stump. And Godfrey could take Jim Laker on a turner like a ferret consuming a rabbit.

Australia's new freak bowler, Jack Iverson, played on this tour. He imparted fierce spin by doubling back his middle finger under the ball. It was almost impossible to detect which way the ball would turn. I played him as an offspinner simply because that was the one delivery he could turn effectively past the bat. The others tended to come straight on. 'Facing him is like someone bowling a handful of confetti', observed one player. Thirty-five

when he played in his first Test, Iverson at six feet tall and
sixteen stone was perhaps the most unlikely cricketer ever
to rise to the top. He achieved the feat remarkably by
discovering a freak delivery when playing with a table
tennis ball. He came to the top knowing next to nothing
about the game. His captain, Lindsay Hassett, would
point to areas of the field in which he wanted Iverson to
stand, never daring to expose the spinner's ignorance of
field placings. But who cares about such labels as forward
short leg when a bowler can claim twenty-one England
victims in a series at fifteen apiece? Iverson topped
Australia's bowling averages in that series before slipping
quietly back to the comparative obscurity of his native
Victoria.

There were hopes that for the first time since the war
our batting and bowling would function properly as a
forceful unit when we went to the West Indies in 1953-4.
Bowling had let us down in Australia in 1946-7; batting
had been the trouble on the 1950-1 tour there; and, well
though we played in South Africa in 1948-9, Dudley
Nourse's side bore no comparison with those fielded by
Australia and the West Indies.

Now, under Len Hutton, the first professional to
captain England overseas, we were seeking a more
balanced performance against arguably the best side in the
world at the time. It subsequently transpired that our form
with either bat or ball played a rather insignificant part in a
series charged with incidents. The series was fraught with
controversy from the moment we landed. The Tests were
laced with tensions, ugly crowd scenes and bad umpiring.
We became aware that it was to be a difficult tour in the
first Test, at Kingston, when umpire Burke's wife and son
were subjected to physical attacks after the umpire had
adjudged the local hero Holt lbw to Brian Statham when
just short of his century. But even that episode was rather
insignificant in the light of what happened in the third
Test, at Georgetown, British Guiana.

Crowd disturbances started when McWatt was run out

in the West Indies first innings, trying for a second run
which would have taken his stand with Holt to a hundred.
He was well out of his ground, giving umpire Menzies no
doubts when he raised his finger. I had hardly started
applauding the dismissal on the boundary when a beer
bottle hurtled past my head, then another, then dozens
crashed onto the outfield. Then a fruit packing-case
dropped at my feet - and in less than a minute the ground
was in chaos with the outfield resembling Covent Garden
on market day. I was in two minds whether to run for my
life or try to weather the storm. In the end I decided
humour was the best dictator of action, so I picked up a
discarded bottle, placed it to my lips, and pretended to
stagger in a drunken stupor. It worked. Hoots of derision
turned to laughter with many of the spectators forgetting
for a moment that the umpire's decision had probably cost
them a week's wages in lost bets on the length and success of
the stand between McWatt and Holt.

   I became directly involved in two bad umpiring decisions which occurred in the fourth Test at Port-of-Spain
on a jute matting wicket. I had caught and bowled
Stollmeyer just before lunch on the first day and almost
immediately afterwards deceived his opening partner Holt
with a googly. He stretched forward to drive, edged, and
Tom Graveney completed a catch at slip. Holt stood his
ground. 'Off you go, you're out', I said. The batsman
ignored the remark, so I went through the formality of
appealing to umpire Achong, who simply shook his head.
Graveney hurled the ball to the ground and in the heat of
the moment I made an uncharacteristic comment, suggesting that the laws of cricket were given a different
interpretation on the other side of the Atlantic.

   The decision was bad, but by mid-afternoon we had
seen its equal when Weekes got the thickest of edges to a
ball from Trevor Bailey which was well held by the
England wicketkeeper, Dick Spooner. Mr Achong again
shook his head. 'What's wrong this time? Even the crowd
heard the snick', I yelled. Unmoved, Achong said

defiantly: 'I, too, saw the deflection, Mr Compton - but I did not hear the snick!' Weekes went on to score a double century in a drawn match that ensured the West Indies would not lose the rubber.

Decisions such as these did nothing for our morale, which was already threatened by one or two of our players, notably Freddie Trueman. One of the tour's mysteries was the distance between two Yorkshiremen, Hutton and Trueman. They never achieved a working relationship on that tour, antagonising one another whenever their paths crossed. Hutton, wearing the mantle of captaincy heavily on occasions, had little time for Fred's tantrums. Len's sole intention was to win the series, thus proving wrong many of those who had questioned his appointment.

Trueman was a handful for him throughout the series. He was raw, naive, aggressive, unpredictable, often trying to assert himself to hide an inferiority complex. Hutton was just as angry as Trueman when umpires' decisions went against us but he possessed an older, wiser head, capable of doing the right thing whatever his innermost thoughts. Trueman would simply explode. What the West Indians never understood was that Fred's outbursts were never intended to question the legitimacy of their births, nor were there serious racial undertones in his remarks. This was simply Trueman talking, the only way he knew how.

The tour demanded a tough, uncompromising manager. We were led by Charlie Palmer, a kind, efficient, delightful man but no disciplinarian. He seemed to leave most of the difficult decisions to Hutton, which Len accepted without complaint but never relished.

We drew level in the series at Kingston, Jamaica, in the fifth Test, winning by nine wickets after Len Hutton had scored 205 in our first innings. I remember him striking a six off a fresh-faced youngster who later revealed some fluent strokes when his turn came to bat. He came in eight or nine to make double figures in both innings, caught

Compton bowled Lock for 20-odd in the second. Somehow we knew that Garfield Sobers would go on to win a few more caps before he was through.

It had been a memorable tour, sometimes amusing, often frightening, but the standard of cricket was excellent throughout. Hutton ended with an average of 96 - an incredible performance considering the enormous responsibilities he bore. 'The three Ws' were in their prime, Worrell's bat flowing like a brush on canvas, Walcott and Weekes producing the carnage. Weekes hooked a Trueman bouncer with such savagery that the ball bounced back onto the outfield after hitting the scoreboard. Sadly, George Headley was past his prime, never relishing the bouncer where once he would have murdered anything short. 'This is war, not cricket', he said on one occasion.

At the age of thirty-six in 1954-5 I was selected for my last tour to Australia and New Zealand, a series in which we won the rubber for the first time for twenty-two years. The achievement has been well analysed so I will confine my remarks mainly to the chief architects of victory. Hutton for his leadership, May and Cowdrey for their batting, and Tyson for his bowling. All four played significant parts at the same time in England's victory in the third Test, which gave us a vital 2-1 lead in the series. Hutton's contribution was somewhat obscure to most spectators and cricket followers back at home. It was not what the England captain achieved in the match, more what he did before play started. Hutton's effort came when he made the decision to play after at first suggesting he was not fit, the background of which Bill describes in his chapter on captaincy.

Frank Tyson's match-winning spell of 12 overs, 7 wickets for 27, to wreck Australia's second innings, was the fastest bowling I ever saw from an Englishman. Godfrey Evans stood further back to Tyson than any fast bowler he kept to in his career. Australia's batsmen had no answer to his speed, least of all Richie Benaud, who seemed to take a middle-and-umpire guard when facing

Tyson in that series. He was put under tremendous
pressure by Hutton whenever he came to the wicket. If a
spinner was operating at the time, Hutton would allow
Benaud to take guard before changing his mind and
summoning Tyson from the outfield for a quick burst.
Miller, Favell, Harvey, Morris - all were at sea against
Tyson's blinding speed. Their frailty against Tyson and
Statham proved once again that there is only a small
percentage of world-class batsmen in any era capable of
playing a great fast bowler. Cometh the fast bowler,
cometh the truth in Test cricket.

The tour served to illustrate that Peter May would be a
marvellous successor to Hutton and that Colin Cowdrey
was destined to be one of our finest post-war batsmen.

The MCC tour to South Africa in 1956-7 was the
moment of truth for me. I had returned to Test cricket
with some success against the Australians at the Oval in
1956 after an operation on my troublesome knee, but
would the limb stand up to the rigours of a tour?

I survived, but whereas I had played the Australian pace
bowlers from the crease in the summer, the wily 'Toey'
Tayfield's offspinners exposed my lack of mobility in
South Africa. So, too, did Trevor Goddard, who plugged
away on my leg stump, tying me down where once I
would have used my feet.

But tours to South Africa were always a delightful
experience, and with Peter May, the captain, Cowdrey
and Peter Richardson enhancing their growing reputations, I was happy to play a secondary role. May started
the tour with four centuries in a row, the fourth a double
century against Rhodesia, whereupon the mayor of Salis-
bury presented him with a gift for his efforts, a live duck.
The bird brought Peter nothing but bad luck. He got a
duck in the next match against Transvaal, a combined
total of 47 in the first three Tests, and another duck in the
fourth. I shall refrain from disclosing the identity of the
furtive figure who decided finally to end the life of our
feathered companion.

5

Captaincy

Bill Edrich

Tremendous tactical and technical changes have taken place within the English game in the last few years, but they have not made captaincy any more demanding than in my era.

The one-day John Player League games, run within rigid guidelines, impose restrictions which leave captains with little alternative but to make the same decisions at roughly the same time in every match. Field placings are more or less stereotyped, set in April and maintained with a few minor alterations throughout the summer. Bowlers also tend to operate to a pattern, perfecting an accuracy of line and length against which it is often difficult to score. The Gillette and Benson and Hedges Cups, of longer duration, test qualities of leadership to a greater degree, but all three, exciting as they are to the public eye, encourage a regimentation that rather limits a captain's responsibilities. Even the Schweppes County Championship follows a formula, especially in the early stages, with the first innings restricted to a hundred overs.

The various mandates regulating our domestic cricket have left captains with fewer options than in my day, although the worrying decline in standards of behaviour, sportsmanship and discipline, especially at Test level, has in some respects placed a greater onus on them. Fortunately the philosophy remains much the same. A captain's first duty is still to win matches, a task which remains difficult unless he has a good side. Greg Chappell's 1977 Australian team in England and the side that

Mike Denness took to Australia in 1974-5 had no chance of securing victories whatever the capabilities of their captain because they were under strength. Whenever a side does badly, criticism is levelled at the captain, although much of it may be unjustified. It is possible for a side to be heavily defeated throughout the year and yet have an able captain, while the converse is equally true.

The English system has bred all kinds of captains, ranging in levels of ability from excellent to awful. I shall never forget the captain of a county from the Midlands, who chased a ball towards the Mound stand at Lord's pausing en route to retrieve his cap that had fallen to the ground before carrying on the chase. Another county captain was so short on tactical ability that he devised a system of semaphore enabling him to take instructions from a rather knowledgeable committee man who sat with notepad and pencil in the pavilion.

Stuart Surridge of Surrey became one of the finest captains I played against. The demands he placed upon his side were never better illustrated than in a match between Surrey and Middlesex at the height of Surrey's successful run. Jim Laker and Tony Lock, the Surrey and England 'spin twins', were in their element. The ball was turning and lifting sharply from a responsive Oval wicket. They had Middlesex on the rack. After Jack Robertson had gone cheaply, I joined John Dewes at the wicket. We decided the best way to draw the sting from the potent Laker-Lock attack was for Dewes, a lefthander, to take the ball coming into the bat from Lock, and for me, a righthander, to face Laker's offspin. We reckoned it would be a lot safer to lap the ball with the tide than to take the more perilous alternative of playing the one which leaves the bat.

The method worked splendidly until Laker turned a snorter through my defence, the ball spinning and lifting sharply. It would have struck Roy Swetman in the face if the Surrey wicketkeeper had not taken evasive action. Fortunately he ducked and the ball swept harmlessly over him for four byes. Suddenly a voice boomed: 'For Christ's sake, Roy, get something behind it'. It was Surridge glowering, hands on hips, in the leg trap. 'But skipper, it would have knocked my teeth out', wailed a startled Swetman. 'Well, I wish it had!', said Surridge. Whatever the merits of Surridge's reaction, that incident serves to illustrate the method he employed to extract total commitment from his side. Surridge led Surrey to five successful championships between 1952 and 1956 before handing over the leadership to Peter May, who steered them to two more titles in 1957 and 1958.

The dynamism of Surridge's captaincy in the 1950s reminded me so much of Walter Robins' leadership of Middlesex just after the war. Surrey's policy of persistent aggression from first ball to last never wavered. Surridge devised a blueprint for success which Peter May, quieter but just as resolute, followed implicitly when he took over. Surridge led from the front, by example, never requesting his men to do something he would not attempt himself. Under Surridge, who believed catches were to be held off defensive shots if fieldsmen were prepared to stand close enough, Surrey developed a standard of fielding comparable with anything seen before or since.

Tony Lock conjured spectacular catches at leg slip that might have won him life membership of the Magic Circle. And Mickey Stewart, standing at short short leg, would swoop like an eagle to wrap his talons round the seemingly impossible. Surridge himself stood suicidally close in the leg trap. 'Catch 'em first, count the dead and injured later', was his philosophy.

Surridge could command respect whether playing the role of master-at-arms or handling a delicate personal problem. Surridge the disciplinarian could be a forbidding opponent. The law governing defamation of character prevents me from identifying the player involved in one incident I heard of during another match between Middlesex and Surrey at the Oval. One of his players had clearly not given him the support he demanded. Nothing much had been said during the match, black looks speaking louder than words, but once the stumps were drawn at the end Surridge picked up the internal telephone linking the amateur dressing room to the pros' to demand a face-to-face with the player. Moments later the player stood before his captain. Surridge's message was short, crisp and devastating. 'We are going to Lord's for the return match. You won't be playing. I'm not having a coward in my side.'

The captains' table of English cricket was rich in character and ability at that time. In 1955, the summer in which Surrey won the championship for the fourth year running, winning twenty-three of their twenty-eight matches, Surridge's rivals were Donald Carr (Derbyshire), Doug Insole (Essex), Wilfred Wooller (Glamorgan), George Emmett (Gloucestershire), Desmond Eagar (Hampshire), Doug Wright (Kent), Cyril Washbrook (Lancashire), Charles Palmer (Leicestershire), Dennis Brookes (Northamptonshire), Reg Simpson (Nottinghamshire), Graham Tordoff (Somerset), Robin Marlar (Sussex), Tom Dollery (Warwickshire), Reg Perks (Worcestershire), Norman Yardley (Yorkshire) and me. Understandably, some captains were better than others, but the opportunities were there for English cricketers to become captains if their talents merited it. Now opportunities have declined with the influx of players from overseas, many of whom are eminently qualified to take over the captaincy of counties as soon as they arrive. Inevitably the task of choosing men to captain England has become that much more difficult. No fewer than four different players led England in the six years after Ray Illingworth left the scene in 1971.

It was significant that two of the top three counties in 1977, Gloucestershire, who came third, and Kent, the joint holders of the championship with Middlesex, were led by overseas players. Mike Procter, a South African, and Asif Iqbal, from Pakistan, did magnificently for Gloucestershire and Kent respectively. And the success of Eddie Barlow, another South African, in his second season at Derbyshire was hardly surprising.

Barlow's cavalier approach is a direct product of Roy McLean's influence. McLean, who played twenty-four times for South Africa between 1951 and 1956, came over to this country in the late 1950s with a young side called the Scorpions, of which Barlow was a member. I captained Norfolk against them in a two-day match at Lakenham, but by lunch on the first day we wondered whether the game would last. Barlow bowled us out for about 100 in two hours, taking 5 wickets for 20-odd. The lunch break gave the teenager from Pretoria just enough time to pad up before he emerged from the pavilion to trounce our bowling for a whirlwind hundred by 3 p.m. I led the congratulations, but shrugging aside the plaudits the ebullient Barlow said: 'Is there anything much to do around here in the evenings?'

One of my deepest regrets is that I did not play more Test cricket under Walter Hammond. I came into the England side in 1938, playing four Tests against Bradman's Australians, a full eighteen years after Hammond, born at Dover, Kent, in 1903, had made his first-class debut for Gloucestershire. The rubber was shared 1-1 but I had seen enough to realise I was in the presence of greatness. It was generally reckoned that Hammond played his finest Test innings in that series, scoring 240 runs at Lord's, mostly in cover drives that crashed into the rails under Father Time. Until then I had relied mainly upon folklore for information on the great man's ability. If only I had been a cricket stump sitting neatly in the ground behind Hammond in the match between Gloucestershire and Lancashire at Old Trafford in May 1927. I was a little shaver of eleven when, on that day, he hooked and drove Ted McDonald, Lancashire's fearsome Australian Test bowler, with such savagery that one of the fastest bowlers in the world was made to look merely medium. He attacked McDonald from the first over, driving the first five deliveries for fours, the sixth to a fielder on the boundary.

He brought the same spirit to his captaincy in 1938, the first time he led England after becoming an amateur. He was to captain England in twenty Tests over the next nine years before retiring at the end of the 1946-7 series in Australia. I played under him throughout that period, making two overseas tours, to South Africa in 1938-9 and to Australia just after the war. He had a profound knowledge of the game, the ability to formulate a plan and then change it if necessary according to whatever situation presented itself. He wanted the job done properly but was not a perfectionist in the manner of Bradman. You had to prise the Don away from the crease whatever the state of the game. Hammond was different, preferring a fight to a match where bat had complete domination of ball. He would say: 'It's too easy'.

Once when a Goddard-dominated game at his beloved Bristol finished early on a turning wicket, Hammond was ribbing Tom Goddard, Gloucestershire's tall and formidable off spinner who first learned his craft while on the staff at Lord's. 'That lot really fell for your rubbish', said Hammond. 'I could play you with a stump.' Tom took the bait and, accompanied by the rest of the Gloucestershire players, they trooped out onto the scene of his earlier successes, the stumps were set up again and for an over Hammond played a series of sharply turning balls with mischievous nonchalance, using a stump as a bat. The 'duel' between two of Gloucestershire's greatest players was the talk of the West Country for years.

Hammond was a genius capable of Herculean feats one moment, susceptible to astonishing error the next. In 1937 at Adelaide he faced Fleetwood-Smith, Australia's left-arm spinner, whom Hammond had murdered when they met each other a year or two earlier. This time the outcome of the duel was crucial. England needed 244 to win with seven wickets in hand. It was the fourth match of the series; England had won two, Australia one. Hammond played forward to Fleetwood-Smith's third ball of the day and was clean bowled. Australia won the match - and went on to clinch the series. George Duckworth, the England and Lancashire wicketkeeper, said: 'We wouldn't have got Don out first thing in the morning with the Ashes at stake'. Hammond was fallible, but had the ability to manipulate a game according to whatever situation arose.

I know that some people, including Denis, thought him aloof, but I watched him closely over a decade split by war and I would not fully agree. He was the perfect leader on the tour to South Africa in 1938-9, perceptive and astute on the field and an ambassador of the highest order at official receptions. And at team parties he was a revelation. The ritual cabaret he performed with 'Speedy' Holmes, then manager of Sussex and our tour manager, was as good as any West End music-hall act. Many a player awoke the morning after the night before with a throbbing brow after Hammond and Holmes had introduced them to a certain 'Cardinal Puff', the drinking game that calls for a strong stomach.

We did just enough to win that series 1-0. The brilliance of Hammond's batting was an inspiration. He grew to love South Africa almost as much as he did their bowlers. Hammond averaged more than sixty against them in twenty-four Tests between 1927 and 1939.

If Hammond had turned amateur at an earlier age, cricket history books might have acclaimed him England's finest captain. As it was, Hammond in Australia in the first post-war series was a shadow of his former self. The rapport we had developed had diminished and his judgement became impaired by the burden of leading a side shorn by war of penetrating bowlers. He became edgy, retiring and irritable, especially when he complained about us fraternising with the Australian Test players.

Hammond was criticised by Brian Sellers at the outset of that tour. Writing in a newspaper, Sellers, who had been a selector and so helped choose Hammond to lead England, thought that Hammond's stern attitude was marring team spirit. He urged him to re-establish the rather jocular approach to cricket he had displayed in pre-war days. I disliked the thought of an England selector condemning his own man but there was some foundation for the remarks. The advice fell on deaf ears. Hammond had too much on his mind to bother about inflammatory remarks from observers. Once first to the punch, Hammond was forced on to the defensive by Bradman in that series, responding to rather than initiating situations. Sadly, a man's final deed is often the one that burns longest in the memory. I prefer to remember the deeds of Walter Hammond the highly skilled athlete that I saw before the war.

It was still considered essential to have an amateur captaining England, and at that time there were some people who suggested that I might succeed Hammond. I had turned amateur just after the war as Hammond had done ten years previously. It was not done so that I might captain England, although I would have been deeply honoured by such an appointment. In the event I suspect I was a little too headstrong and unconventional for the selectors' liking. I loathed drawn matches, preferring to take my side to the brink to achieve a victory at the risk of possibly losing a game.

Norman Yardley was a natural successor to Hammond for the series against South Africa in 1947. He had been a notable success as vice-captain in Australia, playing in every Test and leading the side at Sydney when Hammond was suffering from fibrositis. He had averaged more than thirty in the Tests and topped the bowling with medium pacers that looked harmless but were possessed of the devil on occasions. Even Bradman was called Yardley's 'Rabbit' after he had succumbed to him in three successive innings. 'Lavender', as he was inevitably known, dismissed the Don twice in the Melbourne Test of 1946, a miracle, he always insisted with characteristic modesty. Ian Johnson, padded up in that same match, was less reticent. 'If there is one bowler I'd always choose to face it's Norman', he told a colleague. When Bradman was out, Ian went in - and was lbw first ball to N.W.D.Y!

Yardley led England to a 3-0 victory over South Africa. How different was to be his task the following summer against the Australians. England suffered four defeats in five Tests, some of the blame falling on Yardley. In truth, we had no chance from the outset. Their batting, comprising Bradman, Morris, Barnes, Hassett, Brown, Harvey and Miller, was of a standard above anything seen in this country before, and their bowling, spearheaded by Lindwall and Miller, tore us to ribbons. The destiny of the Ashes was inevitable.

After George Mann led MCC to South Africa in 1948-9 and against New Zealand in England in 1949 Yardley returned to lead us against the West Indies in 1950, but a career that had started so promisingly at Cambridge University in 1935 was petering out at international level. He was the best captain I played under. No one got to know his side as well, a talent no doubt sharpened when he served with the 1st Battalion of the Green Howards Regiment in the war. He took part in the landings at Sicily, a campaign in which Hedley Verity, his Yorkshire teammate and a close friend, was mortally wounded.

Nothing was too much trouble for Yardley. When he was a selector in 1953 he was so pleased by my recall to the England team after a three-year absence that he drove to a charity match where I was playing to bring me the news.

George Mann's appointment to lead England created a record. His father, Frank, had captained England against South Africa in 1922-3. They became the first father and son to lead England. A Middlesex teammate who had shared our championship triumph of 1947, George Mann was chosen to lead MCC to South Africa because Yardley was not available. Zealous to an extreme, Mann captained the side successfully without indicating that he was the solution to England's brittle middle order. He sacrificed his wicket for quick runs on many occasions, showing only once in the Tests, the fifth at Port Elizabeth, the form of which he was capable. He batted just under four hours for 136.

George represented Middlesex with distinction as his father had done before him. His finest moment came in 1949 when Middlesex shared the title with Yorkshire

under his captaincy. Once, at Cheltenham, he startled
Tom Goddard before the match by telling him that he had
had a nightmare about Goddard's 'wicked devil's hook', a
clear reference to the offspinner's long spinning finger.
Sensing psychological superiority, Goddard went on as
soon as Mann came in to bat, whereupon Mann attacked
with such belligerence that the devil became an elf. Mann
captained England twice against New Zealand in 1949
before both he and Yardley indicated that their business
commitments prevented them from being considered for
the 1950-1 tour to Australia.

Freddie Brown, a large, robust John Bull, became
Mann's successor. For reasons of age alone his selection
surprised many people. At thirty-eight he was seven years
older than Mann. Nevertheless, the success he had
achieved in revitalising Northamptonshire cricket had
made him a candidate for the job. He took over the
captaincy of the county in 1949, transforming them from a
mediocre team to strong contenders for the title. They
won ten matches, jumping to sixth place in the table.
Brown led them until 1953, imposing a vigorous brand of
leadership that inspired the county's revival that took
place in the 1950s.

But would he be good enough for England against
Australia, our sternest foes? Brown himself made no
secret of the fact that he was not prepared to command a
Test place if his form did not justify selection. But he went
into the first Test confident of putting up a good
performance, if not victory. Alas for Brown, Brisbane
produced its customary thunderstorms and, batting last on
a sticky wicket, England lost by 70 runs. In the end Australia won the series 4-1, the single victory at Melbourne after
the rubber had been decided representing a breath of
spring to English cricket by bringing to an end Australia's
record of twenty-six post-war Tests without defeat.
Australia had not been beaten since the Oval Test of 1938.
The victory was justly acclaimed as a much needed fillip
to our game at home. Brown's personal contribution with

both bat and ball surprised those who had criticised his
original selection. He took 18 Test wickets for less than 22
apiece. Not bad for a player who had come seventy-ninth
in the English first-class averages in 1950.

Ray Robinson, one of Australia's most respected
critics, described him as 'the hero of the season'. Jack
Fingleton, capped eighteen times for Australia between
1931 and 1938, wrote that Brown was giving Australian
spectators 'unbelievable stuff '. The most original tribute
came from a vegetable smallholder on the quayside at
Sydney. 'Cauliflowers with hearts as big as Freddie
Brown's', he declared.

At times his patience was sharply tested by events, and
I recall Reggie Simpson telling of an occasion on New
Year's Day 1951, when Keith Miller was batting. Keith
went for a big hit but the bat slipped from his grasp and
the ball lobbed gently to Freddie fielding at mid-off. His
attention, however, had been diverted by the sight of
Keith's bat spinning through the air and, to his horror, the
ball dropped like a stone in front of him. Whereupon Keith
bounded across, grabbed his bat and called out with great
joy: 'And a happy new year to you, Freddie!'. F.R.B. was
not amused.

My only reservation about his performances on that
tour is that he did not always get the best out of his
players. That may sound paradoxical but, although
Brown's technical awareness on the field was exemplary,
his understanding of men was never quite so finely tuned.
Brown's leadership was, of course, a holding operation.
He captained England to a 3-1 victory over South Africa
in 1951. Then the captaincy passed to Len Hutton, who
became the first professional to lead England. Brown's
Test career was not over yet, for he was restored to the
side for the Lord's Test in 1953.

I learned of Brown's recall an hour or so before the
team was announced on the radio. I was playing in a
Sunday charity match for the Duke of Beaufort, a great
supporter of cricket, at Badminton. The game was played

on the village pitch, a delightful setting with people watching the match from the comfort of old haywains dotted around the ground.

The local vicar had given an address before the match started, a gesture by the Duke which pleased players and upholders of Lord's Day Observance alike. We were in the field, the slip cordon comprising an all-England line-up of Gubby Allen, Bob Wyatt, who made the first of his forty appearances for England in South Africa in 1927-8 and at that time was a selector, and myself.

Thirty minutes before the England team was due to be announced I asked Wyatt to name those selected. He told us the twelve, and both Gubby and I were astonished that Peter May had been excluded in favour of Freddie Brown. 'I haven't heard anything so stupid in all my life', I said, 'You've left out one of the best young cricketers in England to bring back a man who is past his peak.'

Bob and I are now firm friends but at that time we were not fond of one another. I had blotted my copybook with Wyatt, then a selector, three years earlier. Midway through the Manchester Test against the West Indies in 1950, I decided that we had the match well won and went out with another player to celebrate the inevitable victory. I got back to the team's hotel rather late and long after the rest of the side and Wyatt, resting in a room next to mine, had taken to their beds. Victory was indeed achieved on the Monday, but before we left Old Trafford Wyatt took me aside in the Lancashire committee room to suggest that my batting on the Saturday had been impaired by my antics on the Friday night. I had been not out on the Friday after batting pretty soundly but was out, brilliantly caught by Everton Weekes at slip off the bowling of Ramadhin, early on the Saturday. 'But I hit the ball off the meat of the bat and was out to a wonderful catch, Bob', I pleaded. Wyatt said he would report me to Lord's.

I was surprised to retain my place for the second Test but at the end of the match Colonel R.S. Rait Kerr, secretary of MCC, suggested I withdrew my name from possible selection for the Australian tour that winter. I refused, whereupon Rait Kerr said: 'Well, think about it because it's in your best interests to do so'. I did not play Test cricket again for three years, gaining a recall for the third Test against Australia in 1953, only a week or two after speaking my mind to Wyatt at Badminton.

Len Hutton's appointment to captain England against India in 1952 was a triumph of common sense. He was the most classical batsman in world cricket at that time, an established Test player with enormous experience; he possessed a deep knowledge of the game and was liked by the players. His appointment as England's first professional captain was only grudgingly received by those who failed to understand the social revolution that was unfolding. Born at Fulneck just outside Pudsey, Yorkshire, in 1916, Hutton had reached the top of his profession by harnessing the genius in his wrists to the sound schooling young Yorkshire cricketers are given. Once, in a match at Bradford, he opened the batting with Arthur Mitchell, a flinty old Yorkshire professional. Hutton played himself in before deciding to cut a ball rising outside the off stump. He swished and missed, the ball speeding into the wicketkeeper's gloves. Most of us down south would have said: 'Easy, Len, easy'. Not Mitchell. 'That's no use', he barked. A tough academy from which Hutton emerged later to follow the classical strain of batsmen who went in first for their country - Hayward, Hobbs and Sutcliffe.

With a blaze of publicity and relatively little experience of captaincy, Hutton captained MCC to the Caribbean in 1953-4 after leading England to their Ashes victory against Australia in 1953. Test honours in the West Indies were shared, but the series was marred by a number of incidents that threatened the fine relations England had enjoyed with the West Indies in the past.

I became a sort of aide-de-camp, adviser, secretary and front man to Hutton when he led the MCC tour to Australia in 1954-5. My form had hardly warranted selection but it became obvious after we sailed from Tilbury that Hutton was to make the fullest use of my extrovert nature to compensate for his more retiring personality. He was never an extrovert, preferring to have a couple of sherries at a reception and then slip quietly away. My job was to fly the flag when he made his exit. There were a host of Australians aboard and it soon became obvious to me that Hutton had to project himself more than he enjoyed to win Australian support when we arrived at our destination. I decided to bring Hutton out of his shell a little at a swinging party on the ship, persuading him to sing a duet. 'What shall we do, Len?', I asked, not anticipating his cooperation. 'Do you know "Susie, Susie, sitting in the shoe-shine shop"?', came his reply. Indeed I did and there followed a fair rendering of the slightly naughty song.

After defeat in the first Test, Len expressed to me his concern over some of the criticisms of his captaincy. We had gone into the Brisbane Test with four fast bowlers including Frank Tyson, our great hope, who took one wicket for 160. On top of that we dropped a dozen catches and were beaten, not surprisingly, by an innings and plenty. Len was always quiet, shy, solitary, sensitive. These events drove him further into his shell.

We won the second Test at Sydney by 38 runs, and by the time we went to Melbourne for the third it was being billed as 'the match of the century'. Fine. But who was to captain England? Hutton told the manager, Geoffrey Howard, on the morning of the match, 31 December, that he had flu and was unfit to play. At 10 a.m. I stood at the foot of Hutton's bed in an attempt to persuade him to play. 'I feel terrible', he confessed. He refused breakfast but, ignoring his remark, I ordered coffee and sandwiches to be delivered to his room. Then Godfrey Evans breezed in, halting abruptly at the sight of Len in pyjamas. 'What's the matter, old cocker?', asked Evans. Knowing that Hutton's non-appearance would be a boost to the Aussies, Evans and I used all our powers of persuasion, finally coaxing him down to the ground. 'Don't feel much like it, Bill', said Hutton as we walked slowly through the main gates, heading straight to the pitch. Then Hutton stooped and pressed his thumb into the pitch. 'It's a bit boney, isn't it?', he said, showing his first spark of interest. 'Come on, mate', said Evans. 'All right. I'll play', said Hutton.

The pre-match drama was not over. Alec Bedser, dropped for the second Test, had been included in the twelve for the third. Len consulted Godfrey Evans, Denis Compton and me on whether Bedser should play. We voted against his inclusion because of the pitch conditions. Then Hutton made a curious decision by asking Denis to take Bedser out to the middle. 'I'd like to play', said Alec, studying the wicket. 'If I do, I'll be trying.' Did Bedser ever give anything less than a hundred per cent for England? The decision was left to Hutton. Bedser was excluded. The Surrey bowler made one more appearance for England, his fifty-first, against South Africa in 1955 to bring down the curtain on a Test career in which he took 236 wickets.

Probably Alec's finest performance against the Australians was at Trent Bridge two years earlier when he took seven wickets in each innings, finishing with match figures of 14 for 99 in nearly 56 overs of immaculate swing bowling. Yet what many people did not know was that he bowled throughout the Australian second innings in considerable discomfort. While batting he had been struck a severe blow on the foot by Ray Lindwall and when he returned to the dressing room was afraid to take off his boot in case the foot swelled so much that he would not be able to get it back on again. When we discussed that performance some time later Alec reminded me that immediately before the Test he had sent down 37 overs in a county game against Northamptonshire at the Oval - and managed only one wicket at a cost of 105 runs.

By the fourth Test of that 1954-5 series, Hutton was still feeling the pressure. He asked Denis Compton to open

England's second innings, with just 94 required for victory. 'Pad up, Denis, I don't feel much like going in again', he said. Compton had started to pad up when, to his astonishment, he saw Hutton putting on his pads at the same time. He went over to ask Hutton whether he had changed his mind. 'Ah, yes, I'll be going in first.'

Curiously, none of the pressure seemed to affect his judgement on the field. He was remarkably sharp, always seeking an opening that would put England's nose in front. Hutton had a dry, quiet wit, never better displayed than in the fourth Test when Colin Cowdrey, a fairly good trencherman in those days, was playing some uncharacteristically rash strokes. Play was halted when Vic Wilson, the twelfth man, emerged from the pavilion. He made straight for Cowdrey, reaching into his blazer pocket to produce a banana. 'What's this?', asked a startled Cowdrey. 'Skipper thought you were hungry. You played a couple of wild shots. He suggests you have a snack and get your head down again.'

Hutton would have shone in any period of cricket history. That he should have played most of his Test cricket with such distinction in the immediate post-war era makes his contribution, for me, that much greater. In January 1956 he retired. He had been plagued by back trouble for three years. Len, in fact, was never robust, and even as the England team were celebrating the regaining of the Ashes in 1953, he was still recovering from an alarming experience. He had been struck 'blind' in the first innings of that Oval Test, but only his closest friends knew of it at the time. He told me subsequently what had occurred:

> I think I was around the eighty mark when quite suddenly, without any warning, I couldn't see the ball. I was able to follow the bowlers coming in but, once they brought their arm over, I could not see the deliveries. Bill Johnston beat me several times. The 'blindness' must have lasted for three overs and finally Johnston bowled me. I was immensely worried, as you can imagine, and feared that my eyesight

was going. Fortunately, England only needed 132 when we batted again.

Hutton went for a check-up and as the blind spell never recurred he put it all down to tiredness which, presumably, had affected the muscles of the eyes.

Sitting alongside Maurice Leyland, that fine servant of Yorkshire cricket between the wars, at a Scarborough Festival in the early fifties, I posed the question: 'Which one of these batsmen do you fancy to become the next England captain?'. Leyland fixed a quizzical eye on the two players at the wicket and said: 'I'll go for Cowdrey'. Although the four-year gap in their ages made it much more likely that Peter May, the other batsman we were watching, would ascend to the England captaincy before Colin Cowdrey.

Indeed, it was no surprise when May got the job, leading England in his first series against the South Africans in 1955. He brought to the job the same dedication as Hutton, a wealth of knowledge of the game, considerable personal charm and a tremendous will to win, which had been fashioned playing under Hutton and Surridge, his mentors at Test and county level respectively. One of the tragedies of English cricket at that period was that ill health should dog Peter during his all too brief reign, forcing him into premature retirement at the end of 1961. Yet in that comparatively short time he captained England a record forty-one times, through one of its most purple patches in a chequered history. England defeated South Africa in a fiercely contested series before May masterminded the total eclipse of Ian Johnson's Australians in 1956, a rubber known as 'the Laker series'.

England swept the West Indies aside in 1957. Walcott and Weekes, two of 'the three Ws', were past their peak, and the third, Worrell, was compelled to shoulder too much responsibility while all around him floundered. Rohan Kanhai, Gary Sobers, and a tall, strongly built bowler by the name of Wesley Hall showed enormous promise but were too immature to make an impression against a side led by May that rightly was regarded as of world champions.

So when May led MCC to Australia in 1958-9 after another successful series against John Reid's 1958 New Zealanders, there was no reason to doubt that England would enhance their supremacy by retaining the Ashes. The party was stacked with experience. It included Bailey, Graveney, Trueman, Laker, Lock, Evans, Statham, Tyson and Cowdrey, as May's vice-captain. Wardle should also have been there but, after gaining selection, he was sacked by Yorkshire following some uncomplimentary remarks about his county captain, Ronnie Burnet, in a national newspaper. May was deprived of his services, the first of a series of problems that were to beset him on a difficult tour.

England were given a 4-0 hiding amidst a throwing controversy that was to cast a black spectre across the game for a year or two afterwards. I reported the tour, seeing at close hand the pressures fierce criticism placed upon a losing captain.

May's problems reached their peak when the side arrived at Adelaide for the fourth Test, 2-0 down in the series. England needed to win to remain in contention. The pitch was not fast and seemed likely to respond to the spin of Laker and Lock as the match progressed. Shortly before the start Freddie Brown, the tour manager, announced there was doubt about one player's fitness. We learned later that Laker's spinning finger was sore but a final bulletin on the condition of his hand would be given after a trial net on the morning of the game. Laker declared himself unfit, a decision that greatly upset May. Deprived of Wardle, he had now lost his trump card, whose very presence struck apprehension into the souls of the Aussies after his success against their beleaguered line-up in 1956. No one can doubt that Laker's decision was made for the good of the side. Perish the thought of the player who hides an injury that subsequently costs his side dearly towards the end of a five-day Test. But May *needed* Laker's services, if only to maintain a psychological supremacy over the Australians on a wicket that would not be to their liking. A stronger captain than May might well have ordered the Surrey offspinner to play in that Test.

May himself was to show the British bulldog spirit in the West Indies the following winter. There he suffered from the after-effects of an internal operation. The wound had opened horribly before the second Test but, despite his discomfort, he camouflaged its seriousness with tremendous courage until the fourth Test, which he sat out before flying home for an immediate operation. The injury prevented him from playing cricket the following summer. To the relief of his admirers he returned to Test cricket in 1961, playing under the captaincy of Cowdrey in the second Test against the Australians at Lord's. May assumed control for the rest of the series but no amount of expertise in handling a team and planning an operation could free the Ashes from the grasp of Richie Benaud.

Colin Cowdrey should have been May's rightful successor. He had been his vice-captain in Australia and had undertaken huge responsibilities in taking over when May fell ill in the West Indies. He had also led England against South Africa in 1960 when May was temporarily out of the game. I considered Cowdrey a most astute captain. He does not always give the impression of being a person who can make fast, firm decisions, but beneath that genial smile, kindly manner and charm is a purposeful man who knows what he wants out of life.

He used his bowlers well, was painstaking in his field placing and, in the quick march between the first-slip position at one end to the same spot at the other end between overs, reeled off instructions with a beckoning finger or sweep of the hand that left no doubt about who was running the show. Unfortunately, Cowdrey took a rest from Test cricket during the 1961-2 tour of India and Pakistan. It opened the gate to Ted Dexter, whose cavalier approach to the game and dashing strokeplay were reminiscent of Denis Compton a decade earlier.

Walter Robins, for one, became enamoured with the style of 'Lord Ted'. It reminded the chairman of the selectors of his approach to cricket in leading Middlesex to the championship in 1947. It soon became obvious that Dexter was Robins' man. A sound, realistic tactician, if appearing to daydream occasionally in the middle of a negatively defensive Test, Dexter was chosen to captain MCC in Australia in 1962-3, at twenty-seven the youngest player to do so. The series was drawn 1 - 1 with Dexter enhancing his reputation as a forceful strokemaker and enterprising captain under the shrewd, guiding hand of the tour manager, the Duke of Norfolk.

Dexter became a 'thinking' captain, a theorist whose philosophies could sometimes cloud his judgement. He was for ever questioning his technique with both bat and ball. Dexter's views on what was best for his side and for cricket were often refreshing. His decisions were never predictable. He became one of the young reformers, somewhat intolerant of lesser mortals, but a player whom others could respect for the force of his convictions. He inspired by example, a trait never better demonstrated than in the second Test at Lord's in 1963. England had lost Mickey Stewart and my cousin, John Edrich, cheaply when Dexter walked down the wicket to join Ken Barrington with a simple solution to the West Indies' fearsome pace attack of Wes Hall and Charlie Griffith. 'You defend, I'll attack', he said bravely. The next hour and a bit was exhilarating, vintage Dexter. He cut, hooked and drove with such power that Hall and Griffith were at a loss to know where to pitch the ball. His 50 came at less than a run a minute before he fell lbw to Sobers for 70.

A trifle more patience might have made Dexter one of the great England captains. His reign was brief, drawing to a close rather prematurely when he decided to concentrate on a business career after playing his sixty-second and final Test against the Australians in 1968.

The captaincy of England became something of a

pass-the-parcel lottery after Dexter's farewell. Mike
Smith, the Warwickshire captain, Brian Close, who had
led Yorkshire with distinction, and Colin Cowdrey were
all in contention.

Mike Smith was the first to be tried in a series in
Australia in 1965-6 after he had conducted a successful
operation in India in 1963-4. His public relations and
relaxed, imperturbable style were ideal qualifications for
the rigours imposed by a long overseas tour. In some
respects Smith's credentials were the best of any post-war
captains but his batting, so strong and forceful in county
cricket, was never truly of Test standard. He was
particularly susceptible to pace bowling, a weakness that
was exploited by Alan Davidson and Graham McKenzie
when he led MCC to Australia.

Unable to bridge the gap between county and Test
cricket, Smith survived one Test against the West Indies
in 1966 before the selectors went back again to Cowdrey.
This time the Kent captain lasted three Tests but again he
became the scapegoat when victory eluded England at
Lord's. England led the West Indies by 86 in the first
innings and had them firmly on the rack at 95-5 when they
batted a second time. It is now part of cricket folklore that
Gary Sobers and David Holford, playing in only his
second Test, treated the crowd to one of the finest
rearguard actions ever seen at Lord's. They took the score
to 369-5 before Sobers declared, setting England 284 to
win. The task was beyond them and only a defiant knock
from Colin Milburn saved them from defeat.

Cowdrey retained the job at Nottingham and Leeds but,
after England lost the series, Close, who led Yorkshire to
the title in 1963 and again in three successive seasons
between 1966 and 1968, was installed for the final Test.
Close kept the job against India and Pakistan in 1967, but
at roughly the same time as the selectors were considering
the composition of the party for the tour to the West
Indies in 1967-8 he fell from favour. The Yorkshire
captain was accused of using delaying tactics in a match

against Warwickshire at Birmingham in an alleged attempt to keep his side in the running for the title. The selectorial switchback changed course dramatically again after Close attended a disciplinary hearing and lost the job in the West Indies to Cowdrey. Close's penchant for an injudicious stroke when caution was more desirable, or the occasional *faux pas* when discretion was called for, tended to dog an otherwise remarkable career which stretched from 1949 to 1977. He contributed much to Yorkshire and Somerset, whom he joined in 1971 and captained from 1972 for the last six years of his career.

England won the series in the West Indies, shared the rubber with Australia the following summer but, just when Cowdrey could confidently expect to fulfil his ambitions by ending his career in charge of an overseas tour to Australia, he lost a summer's cricket in 1969. He was tragically injured in May of that summer and was ruled out for the whole season, missing Tests against the West Indies and New Zealand.

By the time he had recovered Ray Illingworth, enjoying his first season at Leicestershire after leaving Yorkshire, was in charge. Illingworth captained England in thirty-one Tests between 1969 and 1973, a period highlighted by England's domination of Australia in the 1970-1 series. 'Illy' brought the same Yorkshire courage and determination to the job that Close had done in the seven Tests in which he led England, but here was a more cautious, slightly more dependable leader. He was a mean captain, not in lifestyle but in the manner in which he rarely conceded territory to the opposition. Victory over Illingworth's teams had to be achieved the hard way. Only after he had ensured that England were safe from defeat would he consider other possibilities. But he was approaching thirty-seven when he took over, a factor which was to have a bearing on the duration of his reign. If only he had come to power earlier we might have been spared the problems that seemed to beset those who took charge of England after Dexter.

Mike Denness, Illingworth's successor, hardly stood a chance when he received the job almost by default. He was appointed after a persistent injury ruled out Tony Lewis, an obvious successor in view of his successful leadership in India and Pakistan in 1972-3. Denness had gone east as Lewis's vice-captain but was seen as a stand-in, not to be considered as a permanent appointment, when the Welshman retired. It was a tribute to Denness's courage that he decided to carry on after a difficult tour to the West Indies where his leadership was criticised. His tactics were questioned, his attitude was said to be rather detached and his batting brittle, especially against bowling of the highest class. Ever the diplomat, Denness refrained from embarking on a slanging match, although he might have had plenty of ammunition to fire.

There was some substance in the criticism levelled at Denness, but from the moment he was appointed to the time he was pitched out of office in 1975 he seemed to fall foul of the troubled seventies, an era in which it became fashionable to question, even undermine, authority in all walks of life.

And so to Greig, the people's choice at the time and the players' champion after his swashbuckling, devil-may-care performance in Australia in 1974-5. He brought to the job no proven pedigree of leadership. Sussex had remained a largely mediocre side after his appointment to captain them in 1973 but there was no denying his charismatic, rallying spirit, which inspired all those with whom he made contact. The big question-mark against Greig's suitability was his tendency to become embroiled in controversy.

He must have made the TCCB wary of his diplomacy at the highest level when he was involved in what became known as 'the Kallicharran affair' at Port-of-Spain in February 1974. Bernard Julien played the last ball of the second day's play to Greig at silly point. Whereupon Alan Knott began uprooting the stumps and both Julien and

Kallicharran started to leave the pitch. But Greig threw down the stumps at the bowler's end and umpire Sang Hue gave Kallicharran run out. Happily, wiser counsel prevailed before the match resumed and Kallicharran was able to resume his innings. Greig, in apologising, explained that it was a reflex action in the excitement of the moment.

Nor could Greig's histrionics in Australia in 1974-5 have been viewed comfortably by the authorities at Lord's. Some of the Australians had long since ceased to extend the normal courtesies once enjoyed in Test cricket between the two countries, but for an Englishman to plummet to that level was a saddening experience. Alec Bedser, the tour manager, ever mindful of the need to protect the spectacle from ugly influences, curbed Greig's verbal exchanges and exaggerated finger-waving antics that so incensed cricket-lovers; and to Alec Bedser's credit, a generally more diplomatic Greig, carefully briefed by Donald Carr, the TCCB secretary, emerged to take over the England captaincy from Denness for the last three Tests of the 1975 series against Australia. He accomplished a workmanlike job, conceding nothing to Ian Chappell's Australians in three drawn Tests before leading England in his first full series against the West Indies in 1976.

Now, for the first time since taking on the demanding and often onerous responsibilities of captaincy, he allowed his new, disciplined approach to slip. His mistake was to state that England would make the West Indies 'grovel'. Greig explained later that the word had been taken out of context and misinterpreted by the media and the West Indians. But the damage had been done. Instead of giving his side an advantage in the war of words, his comment had the reverse effect as the West Indies pace attack went to work on our batsmen from the start of the Tests in June to the fifth Test in August. Andy Roberts, Michael Holding and Wayne Daniel simply revelled in the solar heat of a glorious summer to send England reeling to a 3-0 defeat. Heaven knows what sort of connotations the fast-bowling trio had given *that* word when Greig went to the wicket, for the England captain faced as torrid a reception as I have ever witnessed in Test cricket.

Greig admitted later to have been near to quitting during that series. He was out of form with the bat and, ever the realist, was not prepared to remain in the side simply because he had been appointed captain. England captains of the future might well heed the lesson Greig received in that series. It proved once again that captains have to have diplomatic as well as other qualities.

Not surprisingly, Greig captained England to their first victory under him in the first Test against India, at Delhi, just before Christmas 1976. He went on to boost English cricket further by winning two more Tests, clinching the series 3 - 1 before coming to grief against Australia in the Melbourne Centenary Test. Whether Greig's rather undistinguished record of leading England to three victories in fourteen Tests would have improved had his reign continued is a matter for conjecture. He seemed to be learning as he went along, relying on a boundless enthusiasm to compensate for a shortage of tactical knowledge.

Unhappily, too, his South African origins placed him at a distinct disadvantage. He had lived in England less than ten years when he accepted the captaincy. A decade can be a lifetime to someone from overseas hoping to drive a bus along the Strand or sell brushes from a suitcase in Pimlico, but it represents insufficient background for someone taking an important position in one of England's most cherished institutions. Almost to a man his predecessors had been steeped in the traditions and history of English cricket. Each knew the strengths and foibles of Lord's, so that he was aware instinctively which path to tread if progress became difficult. Douglas Jardine, Bob Wyatt, Len Hutton, Peter May, Ted Dexter, Mike Smith, Colin Cowdrey - any one of them could have given an hour-long lecture on the social development of English cricket at the drop of a hat. With that in mind, it did not surprise me when Greig displayed a lack of loyalty by pledging himself to the cause of Kerry Packer's 'circus'.

Mike Brearley was given a singularly difficult task in taking over when Greig was stripped of the title in 1977. After all, the Australians were in England and Greig retained his place in the England side, albeit minus his 'pips'. A lesser man than Brearley, facing such pressures, might have wilted. He not only rode the storm but had time to lead Middlesex to the championship, a title they shared with Kent.

6

Bouncers, beamers and behaviour

Denis Compton

Can there be a more thrilling sight in cricket than that of a strong, lithe fast bowler accelerating in to the wicket to deliver a short-pitched thunderbolt? Photographs have frozen the delivery strides of some of the world's greatest fast bowlers. It is both beautiful and frightening, depending on whether you happen to be fielding or on the receiving end.

The 'bouncer', which can be pronounced in much the same time as it takes the ball to reach the batsman, has evoked a degree of excitement whenever it has cropped up in cricket discussions. But in recent times it has become more emotive. In fact it has assumed almost sinister connotations, in modern cricket parlance as controversial an expression as 'bodyline' to those who experienced the withering pace attack launched by England upon Australia's batsmen in 1932-3.

Many thousands of words have analysed that tour in which the England captain, Douglas Jardine, in a carefully premeditated plan to curb the batting power of Don Bradman, used Harold Larwood - and to a lesser extent Bill Voce and Bill Bowes - to attack the general line of the batsman's body, backed by a ring of close leg-side fielders. Larwood's speed and accuracy and his short-length bowling made batting a hazardous experience. More than one Australian batsman was struck and, when the Australian Board of Control cabled Lord's complaining at this form of attack, MCC responded by suggesting that it might be desirable to cancel the remainder of the tour. Eventually, after further cables, the tour proceeded.

When he returned to England Gubby Allen, the fourth member of England's fast-bowling quartet, who had refused his captain's request to follow Larwood's example, demonstrated to the committee in the long room at Lord's that it was *bodyline* bowling because the bouncers followed the batsman no matter how far he edged away to the leg. After that, 'bodyline' became almost unmentionable. Its usage in cricket circles was reckoned to be as imprudent as words like 'rickets' and 'scurvy' were in other areas of society.

Greater freedom of speech has broken down some of the old-fashioned barriers, but even in today's more relaxed climate the word 'bouncer' is used with caution. All sorts of ramifications can follow if it is mentioned out of turn at the end of a day's Test cricket in which short-pitched deliveries have been used without control. A suggestion that a side has been over-zealous in its employment of the bouncer can cause embarrassment all round, serious enough on occasions to threaten relationships between the rival Test-playing countries. No subject could inject more heat into the inquests which followed England's heavy defeat by Australia in the 1974-5 series. It was the bouncer, not the other weapons in the armouries of Dennis Lillee and Jeff Thomson, which became the talking point. And English spectators became just as incensed when the West Indies fast bowlers launched a fusillade of bouncers in the 1976 series.

So why has the bouncer become tarnished after many years in which great fast bowlers have used it without much fuss or recrimination? I believe the answer lies in the way in which the bouncer has been used and exploited. The purpose of bowling a bouncer is, and has always been, to unsettle batsmen, leading hopefully to their dismissal. It is a short, sharp frightener, not a ball delivered with the intention of placing the batsman in hospital.

Unfortunately it seems that the shock ball, bowled at most once or twice in every two or three overs, has been allowed to become almost a stock ball. It would be an exaggeration to say that the West Indies fast bowlers, Michael Holding and Wayne Daniel, bowled as many bouncers as they did good-length balls in the 1976 series against England, but at times that was the impression. If John Edrich, David Steele, Brian Close, Bob Woolmer and England's other front-line batsmen had had to fend off bouncers aimed at the head they might have been more acceptable. But most of the short-pitched deliveries they faced were so short that they reared off sunbaked wickets so high that they tested the agility of the West Indies' wicketkeeper more than the batsmen.

The prolific use of the bouncer in international cricket is a product of the 1970s. Things took a turn for the worse during Ray Illingworth's team's successful tour in Australia. The bouncer was used liberally in that 1970-1 series, especially by John Snow, who bowled as well as any of his fast-bowling predecessors in Australia. He knew that he could feed the batsmen as many intimidating deliveries as he liked *without fear of reprisals*.

Snow was warned by the umpires in the Perth Test and again at Melbourne after bowling four successive bouncers to Doug Walters. By the time of the final Test, at Sydney, the bouncer issue had assumed worrying proportions, finding as much space on the front pages of newspapers as on the back. Snow was again seen as the villain. Dismissed for 184, England had the Australians on the rack at 66-4 until Walters and Redpath staged a recovery. The good work was carried on by Greg Chappell, who found a useful ally in Jenner, a tailender, who helped him retrieve the situation.

The partnership was beginning to flourish when Snow produced a bouncer which struck Jenner on the head as the batsman ducked. He was led from the field, blood seeping from the wound. The crowd, not surprisingly, were incensed, and it is now an unhappy chapter in cricket history that a spectator grabbed Snow, bottles rained onto the field, and Illingworth led his men to the pavilion.

It was clear to observers that for perhaps the first time since the 1932-3 'bodyline' series, captains were prepared to leave the adjudication on the fair use or otherwise of bouncers to the discretion of the umpires. The first seeds of a bouncer problem had been sown, so that the problem mushroomed in the summers which followed, to the consternation of cricket boards of control all over the world.

'Bouncer' had become a dirty word at the end of the 1974-5 series between England and Australia. Dennis Lillee had confirmed his belief, expressed in newspapers and other publications, that fast bowling was a blood-thirsty business, and Thomson, unknown at the start, never hid his view that he derived enjoyment from hitting batsmen. Sensing the series might be marred by a bouncer war, Ray Lindwall, one of Australia's greatest fast bowlers, said that never in his career did he try delib-erately to hit a batsman. His words went unheeded, certainly by England, who launched the first bouncer of the series in the Brisbane Test and then found themselves hoist by their own petard as the series progressed.

Again in 1976 England were on the receiving end, this time from a West Indies attack fully equipped. Three victories in five Tests is an indication of the West Indies' overwhelming supremacy, but again a contest that could have been won in a happy atmosphere by a team containing better batsmen and more dangerous bowlers was marred by the excessive use of bouncers.

I shall never forget the sight of England's opening batsmen, John Edrich and Brian Close, under siege for ninety minutes on the Saturday evening of the Old Trafford Test. They bravely defied the treatment they received from Michael Holding and Wayne Daniel. Hold-ing was warned for intimidation and given a talking-to by his own manager, Clyde Walcott, over the weekend. On the Monday he pitched the ball up to the bat, used the bouncer sparingly, and bowled superbly for the rest of the tour. The responsibility shown by Walcott and Holding

saved the series from degenerating into a one-sided
'bumper war'.

To use the bouncer very frequently is unnecessary. In
facing many of the world's great fast bowlers over more
than twenty years, I was glad that few of them resorted to
unfair tactics. 'Manny' Martindale, Ray Lindwall, Keith
Miller, Freddie Trueman, Frank Tyson, Brian Statham
and many other fine bowlers bowled their short deliveries
with care and cunning. They preferred to lull batsmen into
a false sense of security. Indeed I recollect Gubby Allen
telling me that while Larwood was the outstanding fast
bowler of his generation, 'he wasn't all speed, you know'.
Gubby said Larwood's virtues were speed allied to
accuracy and superb control. 'Off the field he was a very
placid person who enjoyed his pint with the rest of us at
the end of play.'

John Snow can also produce a bouncer from nowhere.
So can Mike Procter, the South African Test bowler,
Andy Roberts, the West Indian, Lillee, and Bob Willis of
England.

My first experience of the ways in which a great fast
bowler's mind works came in 1936, my debut season for
Middlesex. It brought me face to face with Larwood, the
Nottinghamshire 'Express'. Larwood had been out of Test
cricket for three years. A bad injury to his left foot,
incurred in Australia on the bodyline tour, had sapped
some of the devastating speed that he developed against
Don Bradman, Bill Woodfull, Bill Ponsford, Jack Fingleton and Australia's other leading batsmen on that
controversial tour. If he was short on over drive when I
faced him for the first time, his length and direction
remained unimpaired.

I had visited the lavatory at Lord's so many times before
going in to bat against him that I had missed most of
the cricket. 'Lol' clearly relished the sight of a fresh-faced
eighteen-year-old coming in to bat, for he let go a bouncer
as soon as I arrived. By a stroke of the fortune you require
in moments of need, I whirled around and hit the ball to

the leg-side boundary. The crowd applauded and, to my astonishment, so did Larwood. 'Good shot, lad, good shot', he said. Next ball he bowled another bouncer which I did not see from the moment it left his hand to the time it thudded into the wicketkeeper's gloves. It came twice the speed of the first one, so heavily disguised that I scarcely moved my bat.

It was an unforgettable experience. His run-up lacked the smoothness of his England days but the final delivery stride and action were as graceful as ever. His control of the ball even in the twilight of his career made run-getting hazardous. He swung the ball in the air and moved it off the wicket with the same control as Lindwall after the war. In fact, in their respective actions there were striking similarities.

Bill Voce, Larwood's new-ball partner for England and Nottinghamshire before the war, was also playing that day. He had a smooth, rhythmic run-up, the ball in his left hand travelling through a huge arc before its release from a powerful action. In facing them for the first time, I realised how difficult it must have been for the Australians in 1932-3. Larwood, who took 78 wickets in twenty-one Tests, could move the ball either way in the air. Voce, who played in six more Tests than Lol between 1929 and 1947 with a marginally better average than his more illustrious partner, could bowl a lethal bouncer that swung in sharply to the righthander, making it difficult to handle for fear of popping up a catch to the cluster of short-legs.

Ken Farnes of Essex had the opportunity to become the rightful heir to Larwood's throne. He came into the England side in 1934 for two Tests against the Australians and won thirteen more caps before he was tragically killed in the war. Bill Bowes of Yorkshire, who played fifteen times for England between 1932 and 1946 including one Test on the bodyline tour, was another fast bowler with a well-disguised bouncer. Summoning exceptional pace from a rather ungainly approach, he took 100 wickets in a season nine times.

We had to wait until well after the war to find a bowler with anyting like the pace of Larwood in his prime. Brian Statham and Freddie Trueman were quick but not as fast as a man from Northamptonshire, who in just seventeen Tests became a legend they called 'the Typhoon'. Frank Tyson took 76 Test wickets betwen 1954 and 1958 including 28 in a series in Australia in 1954-5 in which he dominated Australia's batsmen in much the same way as Larwood had done twenty-one years earlier. His bouncer was the fastest I ever faced and he was never quicker than in Australia, when he bowled as fast and as dangerously as anyone I had seen in Test cricket, including Lindwall and Miller. The ball hammered into Godfrey Evans' gloves, forcing the Kent and England wicketkeeper to stand a yard or so farther back for the 'Typhoon' than for any other fast bowler.

Watching Evans taking Tyson reminded me of a story told to me by Les Ames, England's wicketkeeper on the bodyline tour. Les found that keeping wicket to Harold Larwood, Bill Voce, Gubby Allen, Bill Bowes and Maurice Tate on that tour jarred his hands. So he would often place a raw steak in his gloves to minimise the impact of the ball. After fielding in a temperature of more than ninety on the Saturday of the Melbourne Test, he sank wearily onto the dressing-room bench and threw his gloves into one corner. He forgot all about them until the England players returned on Monday when, as they opened the dressing-room door, they were met by an appalling smell - Les's steak running alive with maggots!

It is immensely difficult to judge a bowler's pace because so much is relative to conditions, but in my opinion Tyson was at least a yard faster than Dennis Lillee, whom I watched from the sidelines at the Centenary Test in 1977. Tyson kept the bouncer very much in reserve, using it only occasionally to catch a batsman by surprise. I shall never forget the alarm etched on Keith Miller's face when Tyson fired one at him in the second innings of the Melbourne Test of 1954-5.

I said to Frank: 'Keith doesn't like bouncers. Give him a fast one, first ball'. Seconds later, Tyson bowled a wicked bouncer which flew at Miller's head, flashing past the peak of his cap - he wore one only occasionally - and sent Keith rocking back on his heels. Recovering his senses, he rebuked Tyson with the words: 'Hey, Frank, what's going on? Cut it out'. Miller scored only six runs before edging a lifter from Tyson to Bill Edrich, who caught the red blur at slip, one of seven wickets to fall to Tyson for 27 runs.

Yet no group of batsmen were more apprehensive of facing Tyson than were England's on that tour. He could be lethal on the practice wickets - the most frightening net bowler I ever faced. Most of the senior batsmen avoided him, suggesting that Colin Cowdrey and some of the younger players should go into Tyson's net. The 'Typhoon' found it impossible to bowl at medium pace. 'Try it off four paces, Frank', we would suggest. He would follow the instruction but the next ball would come down like a rocket. Tyson seemed oblivious to the needs of batsmen in practice, not through any malicious intent but simply because he found it impossible to put a brake on the steam hammer he called his right arm. He hit me over the heart with such force before one Test in that series that I still carried the bruise at the end of the match.

Tyson's success in taking 28 wickets at just over 20 apiece in the Tests was a credit to his skill, intelligence and courage. His attitude in persevering with a shortened run-up after taking a fearful hammering in the first Test at Brisbane was typical of his dedication. Tyson became coordinator of coaching for the Victorian Cricket Association when he emigrated to Australia and in 1977 succeeded Jack Potter as coach to the State squad. He always listened to advice, even though his education at Durham University made him more knowledgeable than some of us passing him tips. Only once do I recall him ignoring advice. That was in the Manchester Test of the series against South Africa in 1955. South Africa needed

145 to win in two and a quarter hours and went for the
runs from the start. Jackie McGlew and Roy McLean
came together after two wickets had fallen for 23.

When McLean came in, I said to Frank: 'Don't feed
this one bouncers, Frank, he's a murderous hooker'.
Tyson, the fastest bowler in the world and brimming with
confidence, said nothing. His first ball was a snorter, short
and rising off the wicket at an alarming speed. Evasive
action would have been necessary from most mortals, but
not this man. McLean saw the ball so early that he
clubbed it wide of my right hand at mid-on. McLean gave
Tyson's next delivery the same treatment and at the end
of the over a rather worried fast bowler said to me: 'I see
what you mean, Denis'.

Tyson was the fastest, but Brian Statham of Lancashire
and England was the most accurate. He rarely pitched
short, preferring to concentrate on line and length, gaining
movement off the wicket to make the batsman play at
every delivery. You ignored a ball from Brian at your
peril. Only occasionally would he slip in a bouncer,
disguising it so cleverly that it brought him many wickets.
Its trajectory would threaten the Adam's apple rather than
the skull. It skimmed off the wicket.

One of my weaknesses was that I never knew how to
duck to avoid a short-pitched ball. Len Hutton, Maurice
Leyland, Reg Simpson, Wally Hammond and other
England batsmen have been past masters at ducking or
swaying. Not me. I would always go for a hook, except
when I played against Statham. He rarely bowled short
enough to get into the stroke before he was through you.
His bowling demanded a defensive shot off the back foot,
nothing more. Statham's bouncer often had me in trouble.
He might hide it in the morning session and then bowl it
first ball after lunch. He told me that he did not believe in
it very much. 'It's a lot of effort for little reward', was his
view, typically underestimating the quality of his bowling.

I am sure that Freddie Trueman, Statham's new-ball
partner many times for England, would not mind my

saying that a fair percentage of his 307 wickets in sixty-seven Tests came from batsmen having a go at his bowling after being pinned in their blockholes by Statham's accuracy. There was a marked contrast in styles between them. The players Statham dismissed in claiming 252 Test wickets will vouch for the fact that he allied accuracy to exceptional pace and the ability to move the ball off the seam. I never looked to hit Statham through the covers. It had to be nudge and push for a single here, a single there.

'Fiery Fred' was the exact opposite in both character and technique. Trueman had enormous presence, aggression and speed and an unpredictability that separates exceptional bowlers from ordinary ones. Trueman would bowl one short, then a half-volley which you might smack for four, then an awayswinger going late in flight. I always looked to hit Freddie for four, even if the best of intentions were rarely fulfilled when he was on song.

Paradoxically, I least liked playing against Trueman. It might sound an odd contradiction but Statham's accuracy made him almost predictable. I tended to limit my strokeplay aginst him, knowing that fullblooded attacking shots were almost impossible. Facing Trueman was much the same as facing Keith Miller. No two deliveries were the same, but in mixing them Trueman and Miller always gave batsmen a chance before bringing them back to earth with a nearly unplayable delivery.

Like all characters Trueman has attracted his fair share of stories, some so vivid in the retelling that I sometimes suspect they are apocryphal. In fact I still doubt the authenticity of an occasion when the Indian batsmen were suffering alarmingly at his hands in 1952. One of them decided his only chance of survival lay in trying to destroy Fred's rhythmic approach to the wicket. So as Fred ran up to bowl he stopped him in his stride and asked if the sightscreen could be moved. This happened several times before there came the inevitable reaction, not as one would have imagined from Fred himself but from Frank

Chester, the umpire. 'Now tell me, sir, where *would* you like the screen placed?', he enquired, a trifle acidly. The batsman, noticing Fred's scowling countenance, spluttered: 'I couldn't possibly have it between me and that crazy man, could I?'

I am pleased to see that Trueman has retained his larger-than-life character in retirement from first-class cricket. Bill Edrich was expounding on the relative speeds of the great fast bowlers at a late-night party during the Centenary Test. 'Kortright, McDonald, Gregory, Larwood, Voce, Lindwall, Miller, Tyson, Statham, Hall, Snow . . . .' The names reeled off his tongue. No Trueman. Bill had omitted Freddie from his list. Suddenly, from the other side of the hotel room at Melbourne, came the words: 'What about me?' It was Trueman looking as mean as he did when he used to take the new ball. Bill jokingly said: 'No, Fred, I'm talking about *fast* bowlers.' Trueman was not amused.

Of all the fast bowlers I met from overseas, two combinations gave me more problems than most. They were Lindwall and Miller, Australia's attacking spearhead for ten years after the war, and Adcock and Heine from South Africa, whose partnership was much shorter but nevertheless formidable.

Ray Lindwall, or 'Lindy' as he was sometimes called, was the finest fast bowler I faced. He was twenty-five when he played his first Test, against England, in 1946. How good he might have been if the war had not delayed the start of his Test career is one of cricket's great imponderables. His arm was a fraction low for the purists, a minor point when you examined the control he had over a cricket ball. This factor was best illustrated to me in the 1953 series when Tom Graveney came in to resume his innings one morning after scoring a half-century·the previous day. Lindwall ambled up for the first over of the day to let go a yorker with an old ball that had Graveney spellbound. It flew under his bat, knocking over his castle before he had completed his backlift.

Lindwall was at his fastest on the 1948 tour, using the odd bouncer to the discomfort of most of England's batsmen, including me. Jack Robertson of Middlesex was struck on the jaw, and my innings of 145 not out at Old Trafford was interrupted when I shaped to play defensively but changed my mind when the umpire called 'no ball'. I hooked, mistimed the stroke, and the ball flew from bat to head. Fortunately, after the cut had been stitched I was able to resume my innings when five wickets were down.

Don Bradman, a strong opponent of the bodyline attack of Douglas Jardine's team fifteen years earlier, never appeared to curb the short stuff from Miller and Lindwall in 1948. They refrained from giving our batsmen the same treatment Larwood and Voce had meted out to theirs but even so, once or twice I thought they overdid bouncers, even though we experienced fewer such deliveries than we see in modern cricket.

We had no bowling of commensurate speed, although Bradman was occasionally subjected to bursts of bouncers against the counties. Ron Aspinall, Yorkshire's new-ball bowler, fed the Don a succession of bumpers in one match, which Bradman promptly despatched to the boundary. Between overs he said to Miller, his batting partner: 'Keith, I hope they don't take him off for bowling too many bumpers.' I was more chary of facing Keith Miller than Lindwall. His bowling was laced heavily with shock deliveries which made it impossible to relax.

Ian Johnson's description of 'Nugget' is the best I have heard. 'There are times when I dislike Keith immensely', says the former Australian captain. 'He can be quite delightful because he can be so charming. He can be quite impossible because he can be so selfish. And he is quite unpredictable because he has a touch of genius.'

Tall, upright and handsome, Miller had the charisma of a Hollywood star. His batting was dynamic, his fielding was superb and his bowling earned him 170 wickets in fifty-five Tests. He once played golf with Alan Walker, a

left-arm fast bowler from New South Wales who spent a
short time with Nottinghamshire in the late 1950s. The
contest took place in South Africa at a time when the
papers were full of lurid tales about the deadly black
mamba snake. Walker disappeared into the undergrowth
when an iron shot veered off course, holding up a ladies'
four-ball following up behind. Suddenly a scream shat-
tered the peace and Walker emerged from the undergrowth clutching his trouser leg 'Quick, Keith, a snake's
up my leg and it's bitten me. I've got hold of it - what shall
I do?' Without hesitating, Miller advised Walker to take
off his trousers and shake them out while he himself
clubbed the reptile with a wood. Miller helped Walker
undo his trousers and then stood back to deliver the death
blow. Walker dropped his trousers, shook them - and out
dropped a little harmless lizard. Miller promptly offered
the trousers and the lizard to an astonished group of
women golfers.

For all his unconventional behaviour, which at times
brought him into conflict with authority, Miller was never
anti-Establishment. Stories about his arguments with
Bradman were often far-fetched, and even if he did
disagree with his captain occasionally, his loyalty was
never in question. I am sure there is a lesson there for
today's cricketers, some of whom want to 'do their own
thing', but fall foul of officialdom.

If Miller and Lindwall tried to knock your block off with
a smile, Neil Adcock and Peter Heine never disguised
their dislike of batsmen when they toured England with
South Africa in 1955. Adcock's length was somewhat
awry in that series, but as a partnership they were a
frightening combination. Fortunately, I managed to get on
with both of them. Heine, an Afrikaner making his first
tour, took 21 England wickets after being left out of the
Trent Bridge first Test. Six feet four inches tall, he was
extremely hostile, although lacking some of Adcock's
exceptional pace. Adcock went on to become the more
successful of the two, taking 104 wickets in twenty-six

Tests at 21 apiece. He bowled exceptionally well at Old Trafford in that 1955 series, dismissing Graveney, opening the England innings, for a duck, and making me fight all the way for my 158 on a wicket from which he extracted surprising lift.

It concerns me that many more bouncers are bowled now than when I played Test cricket. It is difficult for the authorities to legislate on the issue, although the ICC are to be admired for the stand they took at a meeting in July 1976 at which they condemned dangerous bowling. As a guide to umpires. It is a matter for their judgement. Unfortunately pitched short and passed or would have passed above shoulder height of a batsman standing normally at the crease. It would be detrimental to the game to try to put a figure on how many short-pitched balls could be bowled at batsmen. The answer to the problem rests with the umpires. It is a matter for their judgement. Unfortunately the standard of umpiring in some quarters of the globe makes it immensely difficult for the authorities to standardise their policy.

Umpires must also concentrate on eradicating the widespread use of bouncers against tailenders, although I accept that the responsibility for this rests mainly with captains.If it sounds old-fashioned to say that Larwood, Lindwall and other pacemen never bowled bouncers at late-order batsmen, then I am happily a fuddy-duddy. I have no quarrel with the bowler who tries to blast out nine, ten, 'Jack' with sheer speed, providing that the established code honoured by fast bowlers is not breached.

I do not believe that the 'beamer' constitutes a serious threat to cricket. This potential killer is a rarity, raising alarm whenever it appears but not happening often enough to worry the authorities. The delivery must be outlawed but again legislation is unnecessary. Control is in the hands of the umpires. It is up to them to enforce existing laws.

The increase in gamesmanship and the deterioration of the

behaviour of some players are closely allied to some of the other problems. The most serious trend is in the increase in unjustified appealing from fielders knowing a batsman is not out; and unethical, often abusive, remarks that are levelled at batsmen with the intention of ruining their concentration. To be fair to the modern professionals, gamesmanship is probably as old as the game itself. W.G. Grace, who bestrode the cricket stage for almost forty years, was not averse to practising it. Chroniclers of his day have recalled how he would distract a young batsman by inviting him to look at a flock of birds flying into the sun. While the lad was still recovering from the dazzle, he would cunningly flight one of his round-arm slows and bowl him.

The outstanding chatterbox was Stuart Surridge, captain of Surrey. He maintained a nonstop banter, telling batsmen they were 'lucky so-and-sos' if they had a narrow escape. It was harmless and never aimed maliciously. Only once did Surridge rile me. It happened in a game between Middlesex and Surrey at Lord's. I had to halt Peter Loader, Surrey's opening bowler, in the middle of his run-up to request some 'hush' from his captain, perched in my pocket at short-leg.

The Australians have always been big talkers. Bill Johnston, whose left-arm pace bowling was a perfect foil for Lindwall and Miller when they wanted a rest, was a terrible gossip. No one would appeal louder than Johnston if he considered a batsman was out, but if the umpire's verdict went against him he would smile and turn smartly on his heels for the next ball.

Nor have the Aussies been slow in trying to hoodwink umpires. Freddie Trueman was convinced he had Richie Benaud caught for a duck in the second innings of the Lord's Test of 1956. The ball certainly appeared to catch the shoulder of the bat and Godfrey Evans took the 'catch' cleanly. Everyone close to the wicket appealed while Richie vigorously rubbed his shoulder. 'Not out' was the verdict and Richie went on to score 97 before he was dismissed, caught once again by Godfrey off Freddie.

Wally Grout was both a character *and* a sportsman (the two are not always complementary). Ted Dexter remembers an occasion when he played and missed at Richie Benaud and Wally appealed. 'I said to Wally, "You know I didn't hit that",' said Ted. Back came the reply: 'Only clearing my throat, Ted!'

And in the first Test of the 1964 series at Trent Bridge Wally displayed his sportsmanship when Neil Hawke, the bowler, collided with Freddie Titmus who was crossing for a single with Geoff Boycott. Fred was still flat out in mid-wicket when Hawke tossed the ball to Wally. But Wally refused to run Freddie out - which goes to show that even in international cricket it is possible to 'play the game'.

The only occasions the Australians became really upset was when they were convinced a batsman had been dismissed only to find the umpire shaking his head. I had scored less than 10 of the 184 runs I finished up with in the Trent Bridge Test in 1948 when Ian Johnson floated an offspinner past my bat. Frank Chester turned down his appeal for lbw and for the rest of that innings Don Tallon, the Australian wicketkeeper, left me in no doubt as to his views.

But for every Test player prepared to say his piece there were many, during my playing career, who maintained their dignity even in adversity. Two classic examples of this brand of sportsmanship were seen in the fifth Test against South Africa in 1955. South Africa had lost four vital second innings wickets in the space of eighteen balls, McLean and Russell Endean falling for a duck apiece to two questionable lbw decisions. They accepted the verdict, and although unhappy at the time they never allowed their innermost feelings to erupt in a show of anger. My respect for the sportsmanship of South African cricketers increased greatly at that time, for defeat at the Oval cost them the rubber.

The difference between the exchanges then and the chat

we see now is that many of the outbursts in my day were spontaneous, often regretted, and soon forgotten. Now, remarks are sometimes premeditated, aggressive to the point of slander, and damaging to the game. If cricket is to maintain the clean image it has developed over the years, it needs more examples of good-humoured sportsmanship of the type shown in the Centenary Test in Melbourne by Rod Marsh, the Australian wicketkeeper, who called Derek Randall back after the batsman had been given out caught behind during his innings of 174. 'What, have you gone all religious or something, Rod?', joked Greg Chappell at the end of the over. A flash of sportsmanship inspiring a flash of humour. That is what cricket should be all about.

I abhor the pressure that is placed upon Test umpires by some players in seeking a cheap dismissal when they know a batsman is not out. Enthusiastic shouts for catches behind the wicket and for lbw decisions are fine if they are confined to those fielding close to the wicket. In my time, usually only the bowler and the wicketkeeper asked for these. Now, fielders shout from cover, sometimes with the purpose of preventing the batsman from running.

With television cameras freezing contentious moments, the umpires' decisions have to be beyond reproach. English umpires face trial by TV at every Test match in this country. I can think of no other job outside work for television where every moment of a working day comes under the scrutiny of 'big brother'. A daunting thought for umpires.

The demands upon umpires now that the one-day competitions are flourishing in conjunction with the championship makes their life even more hazardous. It is not difficult to plead a case for a salary increase for them, whatever the pay code stipulates. The highest paid umpires in England in 1977 were still drawing only comparatively small salaries. We can be justly proud of England's umpires, recognised quite rightly throughout the game as the best in the world. And I can count myself

fortunate to have seen some of the best - men like Frank
Chester, Frank Lee and Syd Buller.

Chester, who retired at the end of the 1955 season,
terminating a career in which he officiated in more than a
thousand first-class fixtures including forty-eight Tests,
would never have been intimidated by some of the tactics
we see today. He was shrewd, fair and incredibly
courageous in taking up umpiring after losing his right
arm below the elbow in the First World War. He never
wavered, giving his decisions without fear or favour. It is
said that in his first county match between Essex and
Somerset, at Leyton in 1922, Chester was called upon to
give decisions against both captains, J.W.H.T. Douglas
and J. Daniell. He gave Douglas out lbw and Daniell
stumped. 'You'll be signing your death warrant if you go
on like that,' warned his colleagues at the other end. In
those days captains were often autocrats and such was
their power that an umpire who offended them could easily
find himself removed from the first-class list.

Chester was immensely brave under pressure when he
had to adjudicate from square leg on a controversial slip
catch involving me. It happened in the 1953 series
between England and Australia. I edged Lindwall to Hole
at slip, remaining at the crease for Frank Lee's verdict
from the bowler's end. 'Come on, Denis, off you go, he
caught it,' insisted Miller at slip. I declined the invitation,
sensing that Hole might have scooped the ball up on the
half-volley. Umpire Lee admitted he had not had a clear
view and referred the matter to Chester. Without hesitating, and knowing the decision would bring howls of
protest from the Australians, Chester said: 'Not out. The
ball touched the ground.'

An example of the speed with which he saw a situation
and gave his decision occurred in 1950 when he featured in
an extraordinary incident in the Trent Bridge Test against
the West Indies. 'Sonny' Ramadhin bowled Doug Insole
off his pads. Yet Chester contended the batsman was lbw
because he had given his decision in the short time

between the ball hitting the pad and breaking the wickets. Soon afterwards MCC added a note to law 34 making it clear beyond dispute that where a batsman is dismissed in such circumstances he is out 'bowled'. Sir Donald Bradman rated Chester 'the greatest umpire under whom I played'. Coming from an Australian, and an illustrious one too, there can be no finer tribute for an Englishman than that.

Another Australian Test star with a warm regard for English umpires was Sidney Barnes, though sometimes he had an odd way of showing it. Sidney, a righthanded opening batsman with a belligerent attitude to bowlers, was part of Don Bradman's all-conquering 1948 team.

While playing at Leicester, Barnes was given lbw by Alex Skelding after an innings including a six and leg byes which he insisted were struck from the bat. In the pavilion Barnes grinned across at Skelding and asked how many pairs of spectacles he needed and also enquired after the health of his dog. Skelding, never one to be outdone in such contests, penned a note to Barnes before officiating in the Surrey match with the Australians. 'I started it Dear Sid, then crossed out Dear, then crossed out Sid, and started Barnes,' said Skelding. In the letter he explained that he possessed three pairs of glasses, one for sixes and one for leg byes, and one for leg-before decisions. As to his dog, he was sorry but he was not permitted to bring it on the ground. During the match a dog escaped from the crowd and bolted onto the field. Barnes swooped on it and handed it to Skelding. 'Now all you want, Alex, is a white stick,' Barnes told him.

If Skelding erred occasionally, he was rarely taken to task by the players. He even drew a smile from batsmen in giving them out. Once in a county match between Middlesex and Somerset, Arthur Wellard let out a tremendous appeal for lbw against me. Skelding, looking sorrowful, said: 'I'm sorry, Denis, I love you, you know that, but I am afraid that this time you must take a little walk to the pavilion'. How could I refuse the invitation?

Syd Buller must count as one of the greatest umpires this country has produced; and for quiet, unruffled adjudication Frank Lee must run him close. It was apt that these two umpires, who always believed the game should be played to the letter of the law, should feature in a match in which England umpires made a stand against suspect bowling actions. Frank Lee called Geoff Griffin, the young South African fast bowler, for throwing eleven times in the Lord's Test in 1960. By the finish Griffin was utterly demoralised, for Buller then no balled him for throwing in the exhibition match which followed the prematurely ended Test. Griffin completed the tour but was not asked to bowl again in Test cricket.

Charlie Elliott, who later became an England selector, was another fine umpire, and Dickie Bird, Lloyd Budd, David Constant, Tom Spencer and Bill Alley ensure that the standards set by their predecessors will be maintained.

The TCCB's decision to invite umpires Sang Hue from the West Indies and Tom Brook from Australia to umpire in England's domestic matches in 1977 will be the forerunner, I hope, of many such exchanges of umpires in the years ahead. Only by sharing ideas and seeing how umpires operate in other countries will the general level of umpiring, already high in some places, be brought up to the standards set in England.

If cricket is to expect exemplary behaviour from spectators, the authorities would be wise to ensure that the game is seen to be played in a sporting manner. I am sure some of the loutish behaviour of English soccer fans reflects incidents they see on the field of play. Cricket has been a symbol of civilised behaviour for more than a century and must retain an image that is envied by many other sports.

I often found it rewarding to forge friendships with spectators. I cherish many happy memories of West Indian, South Africa and Australian crowds. I thought I had struck up a friendship for life with one spectator in India at the end of the war. I was invited to play for

Holkar against Bombay in the final of the Ranji Trophy in 1945. I qualified apparently on the grounds that I had made a short stop in the area whilst serving there in the army. I was delighted to play, even more so when I arrived in Bombay to be greeted by the whole side, including the captain, C.K. Nayudu, who had first played for India against England in 1933.

Just before the match an Indian merchant and a big supporter of Holkar approached me offering an incentive bonus for victory over Bombay.'Mr Compton, we are very honoured to have such a worthy player in our team. I will give you a hundred rupees (about £7.10s) for every run you score over a hundred'. I reached my century and as I raised my topee to acknowledge the crowd's applause, I pondered on the thought of earning £30 for every four I hit from then on. We won the match and I finished up with 247 not out, calculating on my return to the pavilion that I was owed just over £1,100. 'C.K., where's the club official?', I asked. 'Oh Denis, I have an urgent message from him for you', said Nayudu. 'He has been recalled to Calcutta on the most urgent business.'

I loved the Australian crowds, fielding on the boundary whenever I could. I was fed little schooners of beer in breaks between play by one thoughtful spectator. I noticed that Max Walker, the Australian seam bowler, struck up a good relationship with the English spectators on the Australians' visit in 1977. Somebody threw him a pork pie from the Tavern section at Lord's. He caught it, looked at it, turned up his nose and threw it back with a broad grin.

Peter Lever tells a story against himself during the fifth Test at Melbourne in Ray Illingworth's successful tour of 1970-1. England were one up and Peter went to the fine-leg boundary for John Snow's opening over. As he was to take the next over, he began a whirlwind warming up with his arms, right in front of the spectators. 'I was feeling great and ready to bowl,' recalls Peter, 'until I heard a voice sternly rebuke me –"Tha'rt not playing at

Todmorden now, tha knows." '

Playing football in front of Liverpool's 'Kop' is much the same as playing in front of the 'Hill' at Sydney. I remember the Hill for a host of reasons. One particular gentleman stationed himself at the same place for three consecutive series between England and Australia. He was there in 1946-7, 1950-1 and again in 1954-5. And he was repeating precisely the same message on the last tour I made as he had done on the first: 'Keithy, baby, I love you darling, I love yer'; indicating his appreciation of Keith Miller's talents as a cricketer. On the last tour I asked Miller how much he paid the man to preach his gospel. 'Nothing, Denis,' grinned Keith, 'that's old Roller. He just loves me.'

The Hill is the most cosmopolition group of cricket supporters in the world. Lawyers, stockbrokers, insurance brokers, captains of industry and other men of influence rub shoulders happily with the blue-collar workers. By mid-afternoon few of them could pass an English breathalyser test. During the 1946-7 series, a Test coincided with a notorious abortion case involving a certain Nurse Evans. With Bradman and Barnes well on their way to scoring double centuries, England had not taken a wicket for hours when a wag on the 'Hill' shouted: 'Why don't you pommies send for Nurse Evans? She'll get the bastards out!'

I had a most embarrassing experience in Melbourne during the 1950-1 tour when we were led by Freddie Brown. I stopped to talk to a spectator outside the ground after England had posed for a team picture and, when I came to rejoin the side for the start of the Test, I realised I had left my official pass in the hotel. I was not too concerned at the time for the gateman was hardly likely to refuse entry to a man wearing an England blazer and cream flannels. To my astonishment, I found I had misjudged his temperament. 'If you've got no pass, you can't come in', he said bluntly. 'But I'm playing in the Test match', I blurted, adding the rider, ' - in twenty minutes' time.' The more I tried to convince him, the more determined he became to refuse me entry. Finally, I lost my cool. 'Will you tell Mr Freddie Brown, the England Captain, that I shall be taking no part in this match.' He half turned to obey the instruction and that gave me just enough room to vault the turnstile.

The West Indian crowds were less disciplined, but in spite of incidents which marred the MCC tour to the Caribbean in 1953-4 I have a warm affection for their spectators. They too like to communicate with players. When they had warmed up a little, they loved to test a player's diplomacy by asking more searching questions. They nicknamed Freddie Trueman 'Mr Bumper Man', rising to peaks of anger whenever he made their batsmen duck under a bumper but quickly forgetting the issue if their sweepstake on a batsman's run-getting had paid dividends.

What a shame it would be if the various cricket boards felt compelled to control crowds by imposing restrictions to limit movement inside grounds. Cricket would become boring if crowd behaviour was predictable. Spontaneity of comment and action adds so much to the occasion at a Test match. Is it that serious if occasionally a drunk stumbles onto the arena or a streaker takes off across the ground? Provided such incidents are not allowed to get out of hand, Test cricket will continue to be an exciting spectator sport. But supporters take their cue from the players. If they are seen to be enjoying the game in a spirit of camaraderie, the crowds will respond to their lead for the good of the game.

7

Money, Money, Money

Denis Compton

I did as much soul-searching as the next man, probably more than most, for an honest and conclusive reaction to the news that a comparatively unknown television tycoon and entrepreneur from Australia, with pots of money, lots of cheek and more than his fair share of courage, had signed up most of the world's leading cricketers, including the English captain, Tony Greig, for a series of 'super Tests' to be run outside the accepted framework of cricket administered by the boards of control of the world's major cricket powers.

The operation had been conducted in so much secrecy that, when the news broke, it struck the cricket world a blow of devastating proportions. A thousand news bulletins can flash across the small screen before one makes the viewer sit up, transfixed by the revelations unfolding before his eyes. The unveiling of Kerry Packer's 'circus' plan, later to become known as 'the Packer affair', was such a bulletin, bursting onto the cricket scene at a time when the English followers were looking forward to the arrival of the Australian team in 1977. Nothing, not even the d'Oliveira affair, which led to the cancellation of the MCC tour to South Africa in 1968, had the impact of this revelation. Indeed, if a referendum on the merits of Packer's scheme had been conducted during the first week of its release I suspect very few people would have abstained from placing a cross on the slip. It inspired either a firm 'yes' or an equally vehement 'no'.

The defection of most of the world's best cricketers

posed a hundred and one questions. The most crucial and
searching one for me to ponder, as an ex-cricketer and
observer deeply committed to the game, was whether I
would have signed on if a Packer agent had come
knocking on my front door waving a lucrative contract in my
my heyday with Middlesex and England. Would I have
shown him the door? Would I have invited him over the
threshold in order to sign a document guaranteeing me
more wealth than I had earned in my life? Or might I have
kept my options open, turning him away but leaving the
door ajar in case he returned?

My first reaction to the news was one of astonishment,
followed by increasing alarm as the names of those who
had signed were announced with the solemnity of candidates to stand for a general election, then total disenchantment and condemnation of an enterprise which
appeared to threaten the very fabric of a game I had
played and loved.

Curiously, the decision I formed on the issue at the
outset was the one which remained with me after Mr
Justice Slade had made his judgement in favour of the
Packer circus and against the ICC and the TCCB. My decision would have been to reject the offer. Even if I had been
interested, the contract would never have been signed
because I would have demanded a meeting with the cricket
Establishment, a request that would have been ruled out by
the Packer contract which demanded tightlipped secrecy
from all those signed up. I would have had no quarrel with
the idea of a circus for world cricketers - the more cricket the
better - providing it could have been run within the tried and
proven framework established by cricket boards of control
all over the world.

This is all hypothetical, coloured as it is by hindsight.
Nevertheless, I can only repeat that at the height of my
career, in say 1947, I would not have jeopardised my
chances of playing for England and my county of
Middlesex for financial reward, whatever the size of the
crock of gold dangled before me. Would I have signed a

contract under any other circumstances? For example, if Packer's agent had arrived on my doorstep in my last season of first-class cricket, would I have been tempted? It is feasible that a Packer-type tycoon might have considered my name a crowd-puller, worthy compensation for any loss of performance with the bat enforced by *anno Domini* and a groggy knee. Yet again I must stress that I would only have given the scheme consideration if I could first have gone to Lord's for permission.

I hold no particular brief, one way or the other, about playing cricket for high stakes. But I cannot condone the secrecy with which Kerry Packer and his cohorts conducted the early stages of their operation. There is no place in cricket for underground organisations threatening to undermine the work of the established cricket authorities. I make no apologies for expressing what some will say is 'the party line'. The simple fact remains that I could never have become a renegade cricketer in conflict with an authority which had given me opportunities to see the world at no cost to my pocket and to meet people far removed from the social circles I would have moved in in normal working life. I can draw no comparable parallel to demonstrate the loyalty I felt to cricket's adminstrators during my career. Yet I did face a problem, in 1949, which I thought might bring me into conflict with the authorities if I did not choose the right course.

The Beecham Group approached me through Royds Advertising Agency to do the famous 'Brylcreem' hair lotion advertisement. The contract, worth £1,200 a year then, would help make me one of cricket's highest wage-earners. My concern at the time was that a company's exploitation of an England cricketer in fields far removed from cricket might be interpreted as damaging to the game. There was nothing in my contract with Middlesex to prevent me from signing the advertising contract, only fear in my mind that the authorities would see the advertising as an affront to cricket's image. A neat signature on a cricket bat or boot could pass

without fuss, but would Lord's be happy if they saw my
face looking at them from advertising hoardings up and
down the country?

I decided I would refer the terms of the contract to
Middlesex and MCC. I was not surprised when they gave it
their blessing without a moment's hesitation, and to this
day I am pleased I consulted them. For me it was a small
demonstration of loyalty: nothing less than the authorities
deserved. The 'Brylcreem' advertisement bears no comparison to a Packer contract in terms of monetary reward,
but the same principles apply.

So what price loyalty to country and county in a world
where the need for remuneration sometimes overrules
other considerations, encouraging men of previously
sound principles to act out of character? If players are to
expect loyalty and integrity from those who control cricket
in this country and in other parts of the world, they must
be prepared to reciprocate. It has become clear to me over
the years that the men who administer cricket have their
hearts in the right place, even if they are slow on
occasions to respond to situations. Look in at Lord's most
nights and there will be shafts of light streaming from the
windows of rooms in which men are working for the cause
of cricket. TCCB officials and committee members make a
habit of burning the midnight oil, after a day's work at
their offices in London and around, not for personal gain,
but for the benefit of cricket as a whole.

Yes, they make mistakes. Yes, they could be more
progressive. Yes, a few of them may find it difficult to
understand the demands of modern society. Indeed, I
thoroughly concurred with that passage in Mr Justice
Slade's judgement at the end of the Packer High Court
case in which he said that some of the cricket officials who
had given evidence gave the impression that, though
dedicated lovers of the game, they found it hard fully to
understand the feelings and aspirations of those who
sought to make their living from cricket. Some of those
who govern cricket are immensely more talented than

others, but none can be criticised for lack of effort or
loyalty. Cricketers, particularly the great players, owe an
immense amount to the foresight, industry and unselfish
labours of such men.

What hope has cricket of survival if the bonds of
loyalty, upon which the game has survived, are broken?
Perish the thought of cricket becoming tainted with the
hypocrisy that governs the attitudes and deeds of men
in some other sports. Take Association football as an
example. Played at its best, it is a gloriously thrilling
game, well organised and offering rich rewards to those
involved. At its worst, a spectacle corroded by disloyalty
and shabby dealings.

I have never condemned the English cricketers for
wanting to participate in Packer's unwisely named 'super
Tests', which offered them and their families security. My
complaint was the way in which they cocked a snook at
the authorities by signing contracts in an operation
conducted in secrecy more fitting to a cavern housing the
Klu-Klux Klan than a body of professional sportsmen,
worshipped by schoolboys and envied by men in much
drearier occupations.

The behaviour of Tony Greig, captain of England at the
time he pledged his allegiance to Kerry Packer, is
unforgivable, whatever the findings of the High Court.
How Greig could have allowed himself as England leader
to become embroiled in a scheme that would inevitably cause a rift between Packer and the Establishment is one of the mysteries of modern cricket. He had
the world of cricket at his feet; the prospect of a lengthy
reign as England captain; lucrative business offers as a
result of his success on the cricket field; a good name
wherever he went for the rest of his life; and a possible
investiture at Buckingham Palace on the strength of his
deeds.

He must have known also that the Test and County
Cricket Board were exploring many avenues in their quest
for extra revenue to boost cricket in England. It can be

argued that the injection into Test cricket of £1m capital over five years from the Cornhill Insurance Company was hastened by the spectre of the Packer scheme, but the financial backing by 'Schhh, you know who' of the championship and TCCB contracts with John Player, Benson and Hedges, Gillette and other sponsors for one-day cricket were not the accomplishments of men lacking vision, character and enterprise.

Greig, as England captain, must have been fully acquainted with the desire of men of the calibre of Doug Insole, chairman of the TCCB, Donald Carr, secretary of the TCCB, and Jack Bailey, secretary of MCC - all proven cricketers in their own right - to see that the game progressed for the benefit of the counties and the players as a whole.

Time does nothing to minimise the part Greig played in the Packer affair, nor did Mr Justice Slade's judgement, even though it came out in favour of the Packer men. I have tried to imagine other former England captains allowing themselves to be wooed by an enterprise which was clearly going to be outlawed by the authorities from the start. 'Excuse me, Mr Jardine, but can I interest you in a little business deal?' Douglas Jardine, captain of England in fifteen Tests, had his critics, especially in Australia, but I cannot conceive of him entertaining such an idea. I wonder what Gubby Allen would have said. 'Circuses are for clowns; good day, Mr Packer', might have been his reaction. Wally Hammond, who led England in twenty Tests, would probably have said nothing, yet proving that looks can speak volumes. Len Hutton? He might have said: 'Aye, come back when I've finished playing first-class cricket.'

What of the modern breed of captains, men like Peter May, Ted Dexter, Colin Cowdrey, Mike Smith, Brian Close and Ray Illingworth? Would they have helped Mr Packer organise his 'super Tests'? Each one of them loved cricket and would have played the game in a ploughed field, if necessary, but none of them would have gone along with a proposal which threatened their futures in Test and county cricket and risked their reputations in a game they had served with distinction.

The TCCB were absolutely justified in stripping Greig of the captaincy once his complicity in the Packer affair became known. Mr Justice Slade himself said he could see some criticism could be applied against Tony Greig, who had recruited others for Kerry Packer when he was still regarded as the England captain. His conspiracy with Packer in a lawful but secretive enterprise behind the backs of the Establishment was abhorred by all the England selectors and TCCB officials, who had trusted him implicitly. It was important that Greig should not become a martyr and that is the reason, I am sure, why he was not discarded from the England team for the series against Australia in 1977. If the public reaction had turned in favour of the Packer rebels it would have rendered the authorities' task that much harder in staving off the threat. It was immensely difficult for the selectors to appoint a new captain while retaining Greig's services. In retrospect, I am sure it was the right one.

The historic High Court judgement opened the sluice gates to the good ship *Packer* and all who sail in her. Let them build up a good head of steam. They will need it, for it is impossible to expect the English cricket authorities to muck around with the lives of other England players simply to satisfy the demands of a few men who can come and go as they please.

I, for one, do not mourn the departure of Tony Greig from the England team. The statistics show him to have made a major contribution with both bat and ball to the cause of English cricket since he played his first Test against the Rest of the World in 1970. He returned to England from Australia in the spring of 1975 as a cricket Messiah, emerging from the ruins of an unsuccessful campaign to provide a ray of hope for the future. It was no real surprise, therefore, when he took over the captaincy from Mike Denness that summer. Few observers criticised his appointment, though most of us would have preferred the job to have gone to a man born and bred in the United Kingdom and, more important, a cricketer steeped in the traditions of English cricket.

One cannot expect Tony Greig, Clive Lloyd, Eddie Barlow, Mike Procter and Asif Iqbal, all of whom spent their childhood and early adulthood overseas before coming to England to captain county sides in the championship, to possess the same feeling for English cricket as their rival English-born captains have in abundance. Eddie Barlow, whatever his all-round merits, cannot have as great a love for English cricket as, say, Norman Gifford, the captain of Worcestershire, who was born in Ulverston (Lancashire), or Mike Smedley, captain of Nottinghamshire, born at Maltby (Yorkshire), or John Edrich, skipper of Surrey in 1977, born at Blofield (Norfolk).

I sometimes wonder whether Tony Greig realises how important it is for a cricketer's reputation to remain unscathed. So many things happen at the height of his career that he has little time to reflect on such matters. When he retires and survives on the reputation he built playing cricket, his standing in the community becomes of greater importance. I still feel immense pleasure when people stop me in the street occasionally to shake my hand. 'I remember you, Denis, I remember you . . .', they say. It makes my day. I wonder whether they would do the same if I had blotted my copybook. No monetary reward, whatever its size, can compensate for loss of face, especially in cricket.

The defection of Mike Denness to Packer, which came after the English authorities had threatened a ban on those joining the circus, was disappointing but hardly surprising. The men who joined Packer share degrees of guilt, with Denness deserving less of the blame than some of the others. As captain of England, he shouldered most of the criticism for England's débâcle down under in 1974-5. He received another blow to his pride when it became apparent that another England player, Geoffrey Boycott, had resented his appointment as captain in 1973. Denness was thirty-six when the Packer scheme was born, moving towards the twilight of a distinguished batting career with Kent, and latterly with Essex whom he joined at the start of the 1977 season.

The decisions by Alan Knott and Derek Underwood, both of Kent and England, to join Packer were perhaps the most damaging blow to English cricket. Here were two master-craftsmen in their respective fields jeopardising their England futures by joining a breakaway circus that would clearly offer them money and fun but none of the nerve-tingling tensions they had endured and conquered in a decade of fiercely competitive Test cricket.

It has never given me much pleasure to watch experts in any field parading their skills outside their chosen arenas, and my reaction was no different to the news that Knott might be keeping wicket under floodlights and Underwood spinning his left-armers into a wicket prepared in a greenhouse, when they would have been better employed representing England in Pakistan in 1977-8. I was never one for snooker players doing a stage act, for heavyweight boxers giving exhibition bouts, or for footballers participating in comic soccer matches, unless they were doing it for some worthy charity. It was distressing also to see two players whose behaviour and attitude towards the game had always been beyond reproach showing less loyalty to the selectors than one might have expected.

Kent, too, might have expected more consideration from two outstanding players whom they had helped to make famous. Alan Knott was only thirty when he pocketed more than £27,000 free of tax from his benefit at Kent in 1976, only a year before he risked his future with the county by joining Packer. The money poured in from all directions - from old people digging into their pensions; from ordinary working people, some of whom could doubtless ill afford to make such contributions; and from schoolboys only too willing to give some of their pocket money to 'good old Knotty'. They gave not just for the entertainment Knott had given them but for the skills they expected him to parade before them for many more years.

Derek Underwood, who was also thirty when he received his benefit from the county, made more than £24,000 tax free. His departure to Packer surprised me most of all, for Underwood had the ability to go on to break Freddie Trueman's record haul for England of 307 wickets and surpass the world record of 312 Test wickets held by Lance Gibbs of the West Indies. Knowing Underwood as I do, I cannot believe that he has departed from the test scene without considerable regret. To me he has always been the most loyal Test cricketer.

The most crucial appointment by Packer, of the men he took from England, was that of Bob Woolmer, another Kent player. Woolmer announced his decision after the TCCB had placed their ban on Packer men. Knowing the mood of the authorities, he decided to fly in the face of the TCCB, irrespective of the consequences his career might suffer.

Dennis Amiss, the Warwickshire and England opener, was another player to show little regard for county if not country. His England career was probably at an end when he joined Packer. He had played nearly fifty Tests since winning his first England cap against the West Indies in 1966 and no doubt thought it was a risk worth taking. I am not so sure the same principles applied to the way he treated Warwickshire. His benefit with them in 1975 accrued £35,000 tax free. That Amiss could risk the prospect of not finishing his cricketing days giving pleasure to Warwickshire supporters, who had supported him through thick and then, was as disturbing as many other aspects of the Packer affair.

John Snow? A fine bowler, both for England, in a career spanning eleven years in which he won forty-nine caps, and Sussex, for whom he made his debut in 1961. Snow has never been an Establishment man, so his defection was the least surprising of all.

A cricketer who emerged with honour from the affair was Bob Willis, the Warwickshire and England fast bowler, whose pace helped destroy Australia's brittle batting in 1977; he chose the opening day of the High Court hearing in London, 26 September 1977, to reveal that he would not be joining World Series Cricket. He said his county and Test earnings (covered in part by an insurance policy), together with other revenue, would bring him more than the £15,000 per annum offered by Packer's company and that Warwickshire might also bring forward his testimonial. Willis showed a degree of responsibility that none of those who went to Packer projected. In making his decision he was saying that the status and the rewards within the game were not worth placing at risk for a venture which offered a lower level of cricket than he had become accustomed to playing.

Rest assured, the struggles within the game will go on. Test cricket will survive. So will county cricket. So will the one-day games. The only question-mark on the horizon concerns the future of the Kerry Packer circus venture.

The prospects for English cricket have never looked healthier. There was no doubt that the shortage of money in the English game tempted prospective Test cricketers to look elsewhere for employment, but that situation has been largely remedied. All the main domestic competitions and the Test matches are now sponsored and, with industry and commerce waking up to the potential of feeding money into cricket, the game should go from strength to strength. I would like to see the TCCB creating a further measure of security by devising a system whereby cricketers are guaranteed a minimum wage. They would be graded, depending on their status, in a proper career structure which gave just reward for skill and enterprise. The system has worked for professional football and I see no reason why it cannot become a feasible proposition for cricketers.

It would be disastrous if we adopted a 'one for all, all

for one' system whereby players were paid the same money irrespective of performance. We must continue to differentiate between the stars and players of lesser ability. Golfers of modest talents do not make pots of money, so why should the bowler who comes 123rd in the national averages at the end of the season? Players find their levels and should be paid accordingly, providing the minimum wage agreed is acceptable. The Cricketers' Association, the players' union, is already examining the issue. They are also considering a pension scheme. If a cricketer gives twenty years of his playing life to a county, I believe he is entitled to some safeguard for the future. Whether this would be a practical proposition is a matter for debate between the Cricketers' Association and the TCCB, but I am convinced it should be a priority if the authorities are to create a better life for cricketers.

I shall no doubt be regarded as a 'square' for stating that I put the game first and any income I derived from playing cricket second. That attitude was not exclusive to cricket in my day. The same principles applied to other professions in my formative years before men became more materialistic in their efforts to look after number one. I cannot stress too highly the fun I had from playing cricket. If I scored a hundred, especially in a Test, it gave me the most marvellous sense of enjoyment. I am sure the youngsters today gain the same thrill. I just wish they would show their pleasure a little more. The scenes of jubilation in the Compton household when the Test side was announced over the radio on Sundays and I had been included were something to behold. I felt precisely the same sense of anticipation for my seventy-eighth and final Test, against South Africa in 1957, as I had for my first against New Zealand twenty years earlier.

If necessary I would have played Test cricket for nothing, living on my wages from Middlesex, a generous benefit from some immensely kind supporters, and the various commercial ventures which became possible after I had made the grade. I made a good living from cricket.

Good living to me is not simply money - it is also the other benefits that accompany success in whatever field. The era in which I played cricket, except for the war years, was rewarding in many ways. The same applies to the game today if you ignore the smokescreens that are erected by the more militant professional cricketers in pleading their tales of monetary woe.

No amount of money would have compensated for the opportunities cricket gave me to meet some wonderful people. I doubt, for instance, whether I would have made friends with Joe Louis, the former world heavyweight champion, unless cricket had granted me the opportunity. This unlikely meeting between two sportsmen from very different worlds happened at a sports exhibition at Earls Court, London, just after the war. The 'Brown Bomber' was showing the public his ring skills in a series of exhibition bouts, while farther down the hall I was displaying my technique with the cricket bat to anyone who happened to walk into the indoor net with a cricket ball. It was clear that Joe had a lot more courage than me for, while I fought shy of his flying fists, he did at least bowl a ball at me with an action that umpire Dickie Bird would have taken a long, long look at.

Then there were the charms of Zsa Zsa Gabor, the film actress, at Tichbourne Park, Hampshire. She looked absolutely stunning, waltzing onto the field with the drinks during an interval in a charity match in the mid-fifties. As captain of the side brought together by the late Sir Terence Rattigan, my task - some task - was to welcome Miss Gabor. I approached her as she made for the cricket. 'Miss Gabor, we are delighted to . . .' The words died on my tongue as she planted the biggest smacker on my lips I had ever received, to the delight of the two teams and spectators, and the embarrassment of a star-struck cricketer.

Burt Lancaster and Trevor Howard were also playing in that match. Lancaster might have rivalled Arthur Wellard of Somerset or Jim Smith of Middlesex for big hitting if he had been capable of making contact with the ball. Tall and broad-shouldered, he swung massively with the bat, displaying about as much subtlety at the crease as I would on the stage. 'Gee', he gasped, 'how the heck do you play this game?' Trevor Howard would find a place in any team of mine, earning selection on courage alone. Someone - was it Harry Secombe? - hammered the ball high into the air, right above Howard positioned in the outfield. He adopted an authoritative stance beneath the falling object. Down came the ball, out of the blinding sun, to strike Trevor a fearful blow on the forehead. We rushed to his aid, only to be halted abruptly in our tracks with a stern, 'Play on, gentlemen.'

Cricket has given me a passport to official receptions in government buildings and unofficial shindigs in people's homes. I became friendly with Harry Oppenheimer in South Africa, when he was well on his way to becoming one of the world's richest men.

Freddie Brown, the MCC tour captain, and I, his vice-captain, were once the official quests of Governor-General Sir Bernard Freyberg, VC, at a dinner given by him at his palatial government house in Auckland on the last leg of the tour to Australia and New Zealand in 1950-1. Imagine my horror when such a dignified occasion was marred by my taking my first mouthful of soup, only to spit it across the table into the lap of the woman sitting opposite, who happened to be Sir Bernard's wife. As she went off to change into another evening gown, I murmured feeble apologies about the soup being scalding hot. Later that evening, the Governor-General asked me to bowl to him. He produced a bat and a new ball, and part of the evening was devoted to an impromptu game of indoor cricket across the thick pile of the lounge carpet. Men of his stature have a forgiving nature. I have never touched tomato soup since!

While we were at Government House that night Sir Bernard, who served in both world wars, recalled some of his experiences during the second war. On one occasion he entered a Naafi in full red-hat regalia. A lot of troops were relaxing, some sleeping, some the worse for wear. As he walked up to the counter, a big Aussie lurched across, prodded him and drawled: 'Say, ain't your name Freyberg?' Sir Bernard said it was. 'I thought so', retorted the Aussie. 'You're the bastard who swam ashore at Gallipoli, ain't you?' and gave him a friendly thump on the back.

Derek Randall was thrilled at being chosen for his first overseas tour to India in 1976-7. The opportunity to tour with England must have been only a dream when he gained a regular first-team place in the Nottinghamshire side in 1972. So perhaps he could be forgiven for being somewhat overwhelmed by the mysteries of the Orient. Derek became the life and soul of a beach party out there. Champagne flowed by the gallon, and the delicacies included caviare on thin slices of toast. Ever mindful of his players' well-being, Tony Greig, the MCC captain, asked Derek whether he was enjoying himself. 'Sure, skipper', said Randall. 'The champagne's marvellous but I'm not too fond of this blackcurrant jam. It tastes like fish.'

I was one of the luckier cricketers in the 1950s. Many were very hard up, although they rarely seemed to complain about their circumstances, especially if they were doing a job in the winter. I suppose that Len Hutton and I led the field in the income stakes. Len could manipulate stocks and shares with almost as much dexterity as he brought to his batting. As England's blue-eyed boy, he had many friends in the world of high finance who fed him tips about the stock market as others do 'certs' for Newmarket or Ascot races.

It saddens me considerably that the benefit system we operate is not given the credit it deserves. Whereas people in other professions are lucky if they receive a gold watch at the end of a long hard career, cricket's benefit system is second to none in terms of handouts. Where else are men given a tax-free gift by the customers they serve after about ten years' service? My benefit, awarded in 1949,

enabled me to pocket £11,500, a considerable sum indeed
for a cricketer who, like most other people, had been using
ration books. It is not strictly true to say that I received all
the money. It was common practice in those days for the
cricket authorities to hold back about half for investment.
The idea was to present the money as a nest egg to players
retiring from the game. The money was invested in
government bonds and other safe outlets. Unfortunately
the £5,000 withheld on my behalf never increased in value.
Indeed, the sum I took out on retirement was considerably
less in value than had gone in in 1949. The scheme was
scrapped after a few years.

On the whole, cricketers have not done badly out of
cricket. I am not suggesting that many have wallowed in
riches. Yet even if some have struggled more than others,
they appear to be far from unhappy with the life the game
has given them.

My trip to the Centenary Test in Melbourne gave me
the opportunity to test the opinions of some of my
contemporaries and their predecessors in an effort to
gauge whether, in retrospect, they would have preferred to
make their mark in modern times. The reaction of most
of them was mirrored in one reply: 'No, Denis. There was
not much money about but the fun and comradeship we
experienced made it all worthwhile'. The comment came
from Eddie Paynter, a man in his seventy-sixth year, who
fell on hard times when his career with Lancashire came
to an end. If anyone in the party at Melbourne had cause
to moan about the way cricket had treated him it was
Eddie, who played in twenty Tests for England as a
batsman. Could there lie a lesson for us all in his attitude
to the game?

Postscript by Bill Edrich

The sponsorship of the main domestic competitions in
England, the Schweppes County Championship, the John
Player League, the Gillette Cup and the Benson and

Hedges Cup, is not an end in itself, it is a beginning.

I see a much greater future in the sponsorship of individuals. Whereas a major garage group in Leicester, for instance, might be unwilling to plough their money into the Leicestershire County Cricket Club as a whole, they might find it an attractive proposition to offer a contract, say, to David Gower, the county's exciting lefthander. In turn, he would be given a car and paid a salary to appear at receptions held for clients and other functions whenever his cricket commitments permitted. Far better, surely, to put money on one thoroughbred racehorse with the right markings than on an entire stable, seventy-five per cent of which might be functioning better than the other twenty-five.

The success of individual sponsorships depends largely on the capabilities of players to project their images. They have got to be seen to enjoy themselves, and their duty to the public is to play exciting cricket. I could supply a list as long as a cricket pitch of players in England with the right credentials for any prospective sponsor, and I am sure that many more players are coming through the system. I see nothing wrong in players hiring out their names to the highest bidders providing the exercise is given a modicum of dignity. We shall almost certainly see players carrying the motifs of the companies they represent on their shirts or sweaters. Fine, providing the new fashion is pleasing to the eye and is controlled carefully by the TCCB.

No one wants to see cricket cheapened by unscrupulous whizz-kids from the advertising world, manipulating a vehicle they know little about for their own ends. I can think of nothing more distasteful, for instance, than if Keith Fletcher, the Essex captain, were to come in to bat wearing a sweater with 'Zippo Firelighters' screaming across the front, or Chris Old's white rose were to wither beneath the weight and glare of a luminous advert for 'Pennine Battery Hens'.

I believe that the counties should start tapping a

ready-made source of increased revenue that is there already for the taking. I refer to gate receipts, a vital form of cash flow to seventeen counties. I believe that admission prices to grounds have been much too low for years, bearing little or no relation to the prices being charged by other enterprises offering entertainment. A man watching Arsenal or Liverpool play football for ninety minutes from a seat in the stand in 1977-8 would have been lucky to receive much change out of £2. If he had been accompanied by his son, the Saturday afternoon's entertainment would have cost him twice as much, there being no reduction for children taking seats. For county matches in 1978 counties were charging £1 with juniors at half price.

Cricket can no longer afford to undersell itself even if counties fear they will lose support if the prices go up. If the play is entertaining there will be no loss of support whether that particular county is winning or losing matches. The key to the argument is entertainment.

The reluctance of the Independent Television Authority to cover cricket on a major scale has enabled the BBC more or less to dictate their own terms. In 1977 the BBC paid the TCCB in the region of £200,000 for the rights to cover the Australian tour, a valuable source of revenue to cricket, but scarcely a realistic figure when you consider the many hours of cricket beamed to the nation and by satellite across the world, as cameras recorded England's triumph over Australia. ITA have claimed it would be unrealistic and largely uneconomical for them to screen cricket on their only channel. They prefer to offer more 'instant' sports, which provide a clearcut result in the limited screen time available. They state also that it would be impossible to devote the time necessary to show a Test match starting on Thursday and finishing the following Tuesday if the match ran to its full duration. They point out that only a small percentage of their mass audience would be interested in cricket, a viewpoint that is difficult to challenge.

But that is far from the end of the story. The Annan Committee's report on television and broadcasting, released in 1977, recommended the establishment of a fourth channel, leaving the government the option of deciding who should run the channel and when it should start. If the Home Secretary gives the project the go-ahead, the ITA will probably be a front-runner for the new channel. And if they succeed in their campaign to run the channel, the BBC's representatives in negotiations with Lord's over the rights to show Tests and other matches could well find themselves facing stiff competition from the head of sport of ITA. It is all hypothetical, but I have a feeling the bidding might only be warming up by the time they reached a figure of £200,000. In that event cricket could receive a welcome financial windfall.

No one should blame cricketers for wanting more money. The majority of cricketers become family men after a few years in the game, making it imperative for them to establish some kind of security for their wives and children in the short time a sportsman has at the top of his profession. It took a shock of shattering proportions to awaken me to the importance of building up some kind of security from the proceeds of a sporting life. Having said that, I have always had a greater love for scoring runs, hitting wickets and holding a catch or two at slip than ever I had for counting pounds and inspecting my estate.

The shock came during the war in the form of a telegram which arrived at RAF Cranwell when I was a pilot under training, in September 1940. It came from a most unlikely source of high drama, an estate agent, informing me that my house in Perrin Road, Acton, London, had been damaged by bombs. Strings of bombs were falling when I arrived in the road late at night. I could see the house silhouetted against the sky, and as far as I could detect there were no signs of devastation. The property, which had cost me about £1,000 before the war, was let to a young couple so I decided not to disturb them but to see if I could stay the night with my Middlesex teammate, Jim

Sims, and his wife, Scottie, who lived nearby. I found them encamped in an Anderson air-raid shelter in their back garden. We spent the rest of the night under a solid wooden table inside the house, drinking large tots of whisky.

The following morning I saw my house. It consisted of four exterior walls and nothing much else. No roof. No interior walls. And as far as I could see it had no future. I could not afford to have the property renovated or pay the mortgage from wartime income now that rent was no longer coming in. So reluctantly, the house was repossessed by the building society and I finished up with a settlement of £60 or thereabouts.

That episode gave me a short, sharp lesson on the importance of money, which I have never forgotten. I was paid a basic salary by Middlesex of about £100 in 1937, my first season as a first-teamer at Lord's, picking up another £250 or so match money for appearances. None of us was rich but the Middlesex side had as many cars as any other county in the championship, and more than most.

The first opportunity I had to capitalise on my ability as a cricketer was provided by a reputable firm of sports goods manufacturers, known then and today by the name of Surridge. The father of Stuart Surridge, who captained Surrey in the 1950s, wanted to launch me as the successor to the legendary Herbert Sutcliffe, one of the all-time greats of English cricket, whose autograph had appeared on Surridge bats for years. It was an unbelievable honour for an England 'rookie' to be asked to take over from the Yorkshireman, who had played fifty-four times for England between 1924 and 1935. Sutcliffe's contract had about two years to run when Mr Surridge senior made his approach, so the more I could achieve in the time before I signed up, the better the deal I could strike with the sports company.

That was the thinking, but such is the precariousness of sport that I began to wonder whether I would remain in contention after a dismal run of low scores in Test cricket.

I scored only 67 runs in my first four Tests against the Australians in 1938, and went off to South Africa with Wally Hammond's side the following winter determined to do better. There I scored 21 in five innings against South Africa before hitting the jackpot finally, at Durban, with 219 runs.

I returned to England to the news that Surridges' had decided not to use my name on their equipment. Mr Surridge was justified in his decision. I had achieved little of note at Test level to encourage a promoter to show anything more than a cursory interest in my future. He softened the blow by requesting permission to use my name in conjunction with a new range of bats, marketed under the label of 'Perfect'. I was pleased to accept the offer. The name of Edrich did not appear on the blade but all advertising blurb stated, 'as recommended by Bill Edrich'. I think I pocketed about £100 from the contract in the first season.

With all respect to Denis Compton's point of view, I would not have played international cricket for nothing. The monetary rewards for England's cricketers have never been high enough. Indeed, in the old days of 'pro-am' cricket I had to decline an invitation to tour the West Indies in 1947-8 at a time when I was in peak form. I had turned amateur before the start of the 1947 season and simply could not afford the trip. The expenses offered for the tour to the Caribbean were about £50, some £450 less than I estimated I would require to survive several months out there. I suppose I had only myself to blame for not having the funds to support a trip, but there must have been something wrong with a system which resulted in some players staying at home when they could have been better employed breaking their backs in the cause of English Test cricket abroad.

Happily, cricketers' circumstances have improved. I must hope that the players are aware of the hard work that is being put in on their behalf to encourage greater prosperity for the game. It is a start, no more than that.

8

Reform

Bill Edrich

No one can say that cricket has been unreceptive to change. The authorities launched one-day cricket when the first-class game faced bankruptcy. They welcomed the best overseas players in their effort to make the game more exciting and have given enormous scope to sponsors to inject further cash into all areas of cricket. We must not stop there. The time is ripe for more reform, particularly if the county championship, once the lifeblood of our domestic game, is to remain the most important cricket competition in the country.

In 1977 Schweppes injected much-needed fizz into this previously ailing tournament, but their support poses the question of how much longer we can expect large, influential companies to plough their profits into a competition which has limited spectator appeal. It is obvious no sport can expect to attract a sponsor's backing for long without the public's support at the turnstiles. Spectators go to the one-day game because if offers uncomplicated, exciting play with a result. One of the reasons that they do not watch the county championship is because much of it is defensive - the batting slow, the bowling negative and the tactics devised to curtail the opposition rather than force the initiative.

So how best to win back the fans to the county championship matches? The most urgent reform is the need to scrap the present points system. Only spectators with degrees in pure mathematics or those who carry pocket calculators and slide rules in their lunch packs can understand the existing system.

A true game of first-class cricket should encourage the fielding side to *bowl out* the batting side twice in order to win a match. With this in view, I believe the first-class championship should be played under the following set of rules:

1. The time allotted for each game should be *four days,* starting at 11.30 a.m. and finishing at 6.30 p.m. on Tuesday, Wednesday, Thursday and Friday of each week of the season.

2. The one-day competitions should be allotted the Saturday and Monday of each week and the Sunday would remain free for the John Player League programme.

3. In order to encourage a competitive element which would appeal to the public, the championship table should be split into two divisions comprising nine counties in the first division and eight in the second division with a promotion and relegation system of two up and two down each season.

4. The present limited overs and points system should be abolished and the rewards should be simple, i.e. 10 points for a win and an extra 3 points for winning in three days.

Two divisions with three counties gaining promotion from division two at the end of the season and three taking a drop from the top division at the same time, would stimulate spectator interest.

If the first division comprised nine counties and the second eight, there would always be four or five counties in both divisions in contention for titles, and a similar number in the top division fighting to escape relegation. The interest these various struggles would encourage would be a marvellous boon to the game. Four-day county matches would give the top division sixty-four days' cricket in a season, roughly the same amount of championship cricket they play today.

Two division with promotion and relegation would reduce considerably the vast number of matches we see today which have no meaning. While Middlesex, Kent and Gloucestershire were locked in an absorbing struggle for the championship in 1977, most of the other counties had nothing to play for once they were out of the running. Sussex, who came eighth, and those beneath them, namely Northamptonshire, Warwickshire, Hampshire, Yorkshire, Worcestershire, Glamorgan, Surrey, Lancashire and Nottinghamshire were all in that position for most of the season. There is no shame even attached to picking up the wooden spoon at the end of the season. Relegation? Now that is a different matter.

The plan I have set out would encourage positive, exciting cricket. Captains would have to live on their wits to force a result. There would be no restrictions on overs in the first innings. Sides fielding first would risk more to buy wickets.

The statutory declaration after a hundred overs is one of the worst innovations in recent years. It seems that fielding captains can fall back on defence if their bowlers do not possess the necessary penetration to bowl out the opposition. Indeed it offers little incentive to take wickets. Consequently, the system has bred a race of 'container' bowlers, much to the dismay of the England selectors. The limitation of overs has also contributed to the decline of the spinner, whose artistry was once one of the joys of championship cricket. English legspinners are an extinct species. Not many can be seen in the club game either, because of the emergence of the Saturday leagues.

Thus it is no surprise that without players of the calibre of Bill O'Reilly, Doug Wright, Richie Benaud, Gupte and company to emulate, this form of attack has also largely disappeared from schools' cricket. Offspinners have survived but they bowl so flat that the ball is given little opportunity to turn past a groping bat. Pat Pocock of Surrey can flight the ball superbly but the system forces him to push deliveries through with a flat trajectory.

Our approach to the Schweppes Championship reflects the negative way we run most of our sport. Footballers find their natural instincts are suppressed by rigid tactics. So, too, do cricketers, from the moment they are taught to play the forward defensive stroke in the nets in their formative years rather than a free, flowing off drive.

Better pitches are another priority if cricket is to rekindle spectator interest. Nothing has disturbed me more than the decline in the standard of groundsmanship since I retired from playing. My criticism of pitches does not apply so much to the main Test match centres nor is it meant to question the diligence of groundsmen around the country. The truth is that the rewards are not sufficient to attract the right men for the job.

The TCCB's county pitches subcommittee have made every effort to persuade counties to produce hard, fast wickets that strike the right balance between bat and ball. Captains and umpires report on pitch conditions at every match, marking pitches so many points out of five, not just at the end of a three-day game but at the culmination of each day's play. Bernard Flack, the pitch inspector from Edgbaston, takes his expertise into the field by offering advice on the spot, but despite all the hard work and good intentions the problem is unresolved.

Many wickets are slow, not helpful either to batting or bowling. In some of the smaller counties the quality of wickets is sometimes in the lap of the gods, with a fast pitch most improbable. Most of the problems are man-made. The advent of the motorised roller did nothing for pitches. Groundsmen drive them too quickly and too infrequently. Harry White, the head groundsman at Lord's when I was a youngster, would supervise the rolling, muttering: 'Not too quick, now. Just keep her rolling, just. Just keep her turning over, boys.' The roller we pulled weighed over three and a half tons.

What has happened to the two articles of faith of the thirties and forties that it only needs a lot of rolling to produce hard, fast wickets and that the real trial for batsmen is on the last day? The Lord's wicket in my time was dark grey tinged with brown. It was natural soil, heavily compacted like a road surface. Now it is a light fawn colour with a dressing. The Lord's groundsmen have never used much dressing, even when marl, the fashionable preparation of the 1930s, was employed on other grounds. Sir Leonard Hutton still holds marl in the highest regard. 'It gives a fast, true pitch at the start of the game, encouraging batsmen to go for their strokes and giving the quick bowlers reward for effort', insists Len. 'As the marl begins to crumble late in the game, the spinners are able to turn the ball. It is a wicket which gives everyone a chance except when it is very sticky.'

Nowadays, Surrey loam is the most favoured dressing. Traditionally, the constant use of a heavy roller produced firm, fast wickets. Now, with loam, the rolling only makes the pitch more spongy and lifeless, with the last day a batsman's delight. Changes towards faster pitches might give encouragement to a new wave of English fast bowlers.

The Old Trafford wicket for the Test against Australia in 1948 was perhaps the fastest pitch on which I played in England. What fascinating cricket it produced! Walter Robins, an England selector, was not slow to see its potential. Once he motioned me from the pavilion balcony to bowl a bouncer at Ray Lindwall, thus breaking the unwritten code that bowlers do not bowl bouncers to each other. I fired the next ball into the pitch and it rose alarmingly past Lindwall's nose. Up on the balcony Robbie smiled, indicating to me to bowl another bouncer next ball. This time the ball rose like lightning at Lindwall's head, striking him a sickening blow on the right arm. I was so ashamed that, to make amends, I spent the evening massaging his wrist in Lindsay Hassett's hotel room in an effort to get him fit for next day. To Lindwall's credit, he did not retaliate. But Keith Miller did, with a vengeance. In one over he let four bouncers go at me, one of them striking me on the elbow. 'Don't do that to my mate again, Bill!', warned Miller. Don Bradman showed little sympathy either. 'Sorry about that, Bill,' he beamed, 'but when the boys get a little excited, I can't control them.'

I recall reading a comment on the state of county cricket by Gubby Allen. He wrote:

> It would appear that genius is more rare nowadays and, what is still more disturbing, many players have not got that spirit of adventure and daring which in days gone by made the game a so much better spectacle than it is today. The standard of bowling has probably deteriorated but I beg to suggest that this deterioration has coincided with the advent of the all-too-clever groundsmen and his modern contrivances.

Gubby's fears were expressed under the heading 'A Case For More Natural Wickets', in the seventy-fifth edition of Wisden, published in 1938. They are as relevant today as they were then.

I hope that the men who run our game today will not underestimate the demands of those who follow cricket. It has long been my view that spectators rarely watch a match simply to see their side win. A hundred from the bat of Viv Richards, the West Indian Test star who plays for Somerset, can be just as exciting to spectators at Maidstone or Derby as it is to those at Taunton. It is not the colour of a player's cap which matters in cricket. It is the way in which he plays the game. A batsman tearing a new-ball attack to shreds is a joy to behold whichever side he plays for. Similarly, a spinner curving his deliveries onto a nagging spot, or an outfielder snaking round the boundary to cut off a stream of shots, are sights which also give immense pleasure. If they come from a player in the other side, no matter - the onlookers have been entertained.

Some professional sportsmen have become obsessed with the desire to win. Soccer, in particular, passed through one of the most inglorious chapters in its history after England won the World Cup in 1966. The England team continued to win matches long after clinching the

World Cup. Officials were happy. The players celebrated
their victories. Only the spectators questioned the exercise, complaining justifiably that while England were
winning the players were not providing pleasure.
Sport is *not* just about winning. The way in which teams
achieve their victories matters more to the public. Win by
all means - but win attractively.

The game of cricket has always mattered more to me
than figures and results. It was not the statistics of Stan
McCabe's 232 runs for Australia in two hundred and thirty
minutes at Trent Bridge in 1938 which thrilled me, but the
grand manner in which he scored the runs. Don Bradman,
in fact, urged his team not to miss a ball of it. 'You will
never see another innings like it', he told them.

Was it by four goals to three that Blackpool beat Bolton
Wanderers in the 1953 FA Cup Final? Who cares? Of
much greater significance was the manner in which
success was achieved. Will anyone who was fortunate
enough to be there or at home watching the game on
television forget the sinuous dribble which took Stanley
Matthews through Bolton's left flank to lay on the winning
goal?

In some sports cold figures have a major bearing on an
occasion. For instance, split seconds were of incalculable
importance to Roger Bannister's four-minute mile at
Oxford in 1954. Yet, even then, the man's blind courage
was as stimulating to the audience as the barrier he
breached. Would he do it? Would he? Would he? Yes, he
was there! The tortured face; the agonised body chesting
the tape; the exhaustion of an athlete wondering whether
his lungs would ever fill up again. They were the
memories burned on the mind for posterity. Bannister's
face told just as big a story as the clock face at the finishing
tape.

Great matches and great moments on the cricket field
remain in our minds long after the results have gone into
the history books. Only a cricket follower with a brilliantly
incisive head for figures could reel off the result of a

championship match between Sussex and Middlesex at
Hove in 1952. Yet it might not take that much effort to jog
the minds of spectators with heads for exciting events. I
doubt whether any of those in the crowd that day will have
forgotten the gripping climax to the match.

Middlesex had been set to score 216 for victory and we
were coasting towards the target. When I claimed the
extra half-hour we needed just 49 runs to win with seven
wickets in hand. Then Cornford and Thomson, the Sussex
fast-medium bowlers, went to work, and took five wickets
between them for 10 runs and Sussex gained a remarkable
victory by 15 runs.

My point in recalling this match is not to reflect on the
grand finale but to demonstrate the way in which the
match was fought, and could be fought again, if our
cricketers adopt the right attitude. With my last pair at the
wicket, Jack Young and Alan Moss, I beckoned to Jack
from the pavilion to have a go for victory rather than shut
up shop. He smote a lovely four over mid-off's head but,
in making another attacking shot, was caught by James
Langridge off Thomson's bowling on the third ball of the
last over. Both sides received an ovation from the crowd
and the occasion was made complete when the Duke of
Norfolk came into the Middlesex dressing room to say:
'What a magnificent game of cricket. Thank you, gentlemen.' We drove home that evening feeling we had won the
championship. More important, the crowd loved every
minute of the entertainment.

That is the spirit I hope we shall soon see rekindled. I
hope to see English batsmen playing positive, responsible,
entertaining cricket. It is not an invitation to them to
throw away their wickets, simply to advocate a brighter
approach than we have been accustomed to in recent
years - for the benefit both of spectators and themselves.
For if fans start clamouring for seats, not just at the
one-day games but also at championship matches, the
players will reap some of the financial rewards they are
seeking. Viv Richards, Clive Lloyd and Barry Richards

play the type of cricket all players must seek to emulate. Techniques and skills alone do not set them head and shoulders above most of their contemporaries. It is their will to entertain from the moment they arrive on the field to the time they depart.

It should take no first-class batsman more than thirty minutes to acclimatise to light and pace of wicket at the start of an innings, providing he has had a fair proportion of the strike. From then, his objective should be to score runs from every ball he receives. Yes, every ball. The odds against him succeeding are high, but if the approach is right there will be no shortage of entertainment. No one blames a batsman for slow scoring on a difficult wicket or against a clever attack with the ball doing a bit.

I saw Denis Compton murder bowling of the highest class in his heyday. Was it not Arthur Wellard, that smiter of sixes and good fast bowler of Somerset, who threw his hands despairingly to the heavens during an assault by Denis in a championship match at Lord's after the war? Denis and I had put on more than four hundred runs against Somerset in a sustained attack that persuaded Arthur to resort to offspinners - he bowled them well - after his swing bowling had failed to stem the run-flow. It made no difference, and after one savage burst of runs from Denis' bat, Wellard turned to him and enquired, 'Where the hell do I bowl the next to you?' The modern player I have seen come nearest to Denis when he was in the mood for fast scoring is Viv Richards, followed closely by Clive Lloyd. Bowl them half-volleys on the off stump at your peril, even if they are in the opening over of a Test.

Don Bradman had the capacity to take an attack to pieces, sometimes foiling a bowler's attempts to peg away outside the off stump to a packed off-side field by putting his left leg down the wicket to sweep the ball across his body to the boundary by the square-leg umpire.

One of the pitfalls in examining cricket is to believe that everything that happened yesterday was better than what happened today. Nevertheless, I cannot be shaken from my belief that there were more world-class batsmen playing first-class cricket when I came into the game than there are in the contemporary scene. But fortunately the present situation does not discourage me from hoping that the stirring performance of yesteryear will be emulated again. My hope is that the TCCB, in conjunction with the National Cricket Association and the English Schools' Cricket Association, will liaise more closely with the Department of Education and Science on the question of cricket in schools. If money is so tight that schools are not permitted the luxury of a master to teach cricket, perhaps a team of three or four coaches under the guidance of the NCA's national coaches in the North, Midlands and south would visit schools in their areas on a 'flying doctor' basis.

Open spaces continue to be taken up for development so there is no reason to think that we shall have more sports facilities available to youngsters in the next decade or so. Which is all the more reason why we should make the most of our existing facilities. I want to see school playing fields utilised to their full capacities, not just in term time but also in holiday periods. Children should be encouraged to make the fullest use of their school's recreation facilities. Far too many youngsters are not being given the opportunities their cricket talents deserve.

Inflation has largely curbed the Sports Council's ambitious plans to establish a network of sports centres all over the country. They are looking for buildings already in existence that can be renovated and turned into sports halls. Cricket grounds, empty in winter months, might have the kind of facilities the Sports Council are seeking. The eyesight, physique and technique of batsmen playing today is every bit as good as in my day. Where cricketers seem to have fallen down a little is in application and attitude.

So far as I know there have been no statistics produced to indicate the effect that rival sports in schools have had on the supply of young players to the game. I cannot help

wondering, though, whether cricket is being forced to take
a back seat in some schools where volley-ball, basket-ball,
tennis, athletics, badminton and other pursuits seem to
take precedence. Nowadays there is a multitude of sports
to attract a youngster's attention. Many teachers prefer
small-sided games to those involving eleven a side.
Another disturbing aspect is that, whereas most of the
public schools still have qualified cricket coaches on their
staffs, the state schools employ PE teachers skilled in many
tracksuit sports but rarely cricket. I have noticed this
trend in Norfolk, my native county which I visit regularly,
and I am sure the situation exists elsewhere. Indeed,
many state schools have no one to teach cricket.

Teachers' training colleges do next to nothing to
produce cricket coaches with MCC coaching badges, and
even Loughborough College, steeped as it is in sporting
traditions, is not known for producing young men qualified
to teach the cover drive or outswing bowling. The accent
there is on individual sports. MCC and the Inner London
Education Authority have already shown a lead to the rest
of the country in cooperating over the new £150,000
indoor school on the nursery ground at Lord's. There are
seven nets of which the ILEA have said they will make the
fullest use. At the moment there are no cricket facilities of
any kind at some primary and secondary schools in the
London area.

Looking ahead I anticipate that by the year 2000 the ICC
will control a world cup competition comparable in quality
of play, if not in numerical strength of competing nations,
to the Federation of International Football Associations'
tournament. I can see travel agents offering package
holidays to cricket enthusiasts flocking to a world cup
event played every four years. The World Cup of 1975, in
which the West Indies became the champions, was a start.
The public's response to a tournament of one-day matches
was encouraging, and both the cricket authorities and the
Prudential Assurance Company, sponsors of the Cup,
were delighted with the publicity and prestige it generated.

A natural extension of that idea would be to run a World Cup of five-day Test matches in a competition lasting three or four weeks in one of the major Test-playing counties. If Australia was selected, the games could be staged in Sydney, Melbourne, Adelaide, Perth and Brisbane. India is another nation that would respond enthusiastically if chosen as the venue for a gathering of the world's finest cricketers. They have a love for cricket bordering on the fanatical, and crowds in Calcutta, Bombay and Madras, their major centres, are so enormous that a World Cup would be a sell-out weeks in advance. I once asked an Indian player why spectators took so much interest in me after a game I played there just after retiring. One had hold of my sweater, another was touching my shirt collar, another tugging the sleeve of my shirt. 'Are they angry?' I asked. 'Oh, no', said the player. 'Test cricketers are gods. You are deeply honoured.'

The repercussions of the Kerry Packer case are still being felt. I do not intend to involve myself in specific issues except to say that, if ever cricket sells itself to the highest bidders, the game is doomed. Cricket's traditions, established over very many years, are respected by the vast majority. It is not a hobby-horse for the uninitiated wishing to use the game as a vehicle for making money quickly. My fervent hope is that, long after the reverberations of the Packer affair have ceased, cricket will still be fun to play and to watch.

Index

172